ATHLETE FINANCE

ATHLETE FINANCE

AN ATHLETE'S GUIDE TO FINANCIAL PLANNING, MANAGING CASH FLOW, AVOIDING DEBT, SMART INVESTING, AND RETIREMENT PLANNING

HADLEY MANNINGS

© **Copyright 2020 - All rights reserved.**

The content contained within this book may not be reproduced, duplicated or transmitted without direct written permission from the author or the publisher.

Under no circumstances will any blame or legal responsibility be held against the publisher, or author, for any damages, reparation, or monetary loss due to the information contained within this book, either directly or indirectly.

Legal Notice:

This book is copyright protected. It is only for personal use. You cannot amend, distribute, sell, use, quote or paraphrase any part, or the content within this book, without the consent of the author or publisher.

Disclaimer Notice:

Please note the information contained within this document is for educational and entertainment purposes only. All effort has been executed to present accurate, up to date, reliable, complete information. No warranties of any kind are declared or implied. Readers acknowledge that the author is not engaged in the rendering of legal, financial, medical or professional advice. The content within this book has been derived from various sources. Please consult a licensed professional before attempting any techniques outlined in this book.

By reading this document, the reader agrees that under no circumstances is the author responsible for any losses, direct or indirect, that are incurred as a result of the use of the information contained within this document, including, but not limited to, errors, omissions, or inaccuracies.

My brain . . . it cannot process failure. It will not process failure. Because if I sit there and have to face myself and tell myself, 'You're a failure' . . . I think that's almost worse than death.

—KOBE BRYANT

CONTENTS

Bonus Content	ix
Introduction	xi
1. Assets and Liabilities	1
2. Managing Cash Flow	20
3. Debt	34
4. Investments	49
5. Retirement Planning	78
6. Taxes	92
7. Legal Help, Athlete Image Entities, and Financial Advisors	104
Afterword	115
What's Next?	117
Also by Hadley Mannings	119
Sources and Bibliography	121

Bonus Content

Thank for you purchasing Athlete Finance! Get this additional book about Athlete Motivation 100% free.

Many others have already received this free book as well as other full length books—all 100% free. If you want insider access plus Athlete Motivation, scan the QR code below with your smartphone camera.

INTRODUCTION

Athletes have many things going on in their lives. They need to manage their training regimen, devote time to healing, and pay special attention to nutrition. In the midst of all this, paying attention to your finances seems impossible. Besides, who has the time to understand those complicated financial terms and conditions?

I'm here to tell you that managing your finances is an essential life skill. Think of it as being as important as swimming or as learning how to interact with other people. It's a basic life skill that is, unfortunately, never prioritized in our education systems. We learn all kinds of useless facts but never learn about essential subjects such as personal finance, taxes, and estate planning.

You might have read other books on personal finance and might have found them difficult to follow. This book is not going to throw complicated jargon at you. Instead, I'm going to break everything down into bite-sized pieces so that you can quickly understand what the deal is with personal finance. It is a deep subject, but do not be intimidated by it. The fact is that most personal finance education isn't geared towards helping common folks understand how their money works.

It's mostly aimed at helping financial advisors promote new products to their clients and better understand new financial rules and regulations. There are exceptions, of course. These exceptions are usually aimed at people with regular jobs who have time left over to devote to analyzing their finances. As an athlete, you don't have the same amount of time.

For starters, you need to train and recover. Recovery is all-important when you're pushing yourself to your physical limit, and your training regimen probably takes up most of your day. Regular people have the luxury of calling it quits from their job at five in the evening, but you don't have this luxury. Does this mean understanding your finances is out of the question?

Hardly. What you need is an easy-to-follow framework that will help you instantly decide whether you're on the right path or whether you need to change a few things up. That's what I'm going to give you in this book. To analyze your finances, you need first to understand what assets and liabilities are. Consider this personal finance 101. Without understanding these basic concepts, it's going to be tough for you to figure out the rest of your money.

Suppose you've tried to educate yourself about money previously. In that case, you might have found that all the solutions and products that are available cause your mind to go into overdrive, and you don't know which ones to pick. Financial advisors do a great job of explaining what a product does to their clients. However, very few of them take the time to explain why that product is a good choice in terms of assets and liabilities.

In this book, I'm going to help you understand how you can easily compare products to one another and determine whether it's a good investment for you or not. If you happen to be flush with cash, you might have friends and family asking you for money. This is especially the case if you grew up in a low-income household. It's great that you can support those around how.

However, you're the one that is earning money, and you have final say over it. You need to treat your money with a certain mindset. In this book, you're going to learn what that mindset is and how you can implement it in your life. I must warn you that this will be uncomfortable at first. However, much like pushing yourself to your limits is challenging and uncomfortable; it's also necessary.

Some athletes find themselves in the unfortunate position of carrying high levels of debt. Debt is a burden that will put the brakes on any of your life's ambitions. Getting rid of it is crucial for success. It doesn't matter whether your debt is small or large. Assuming any debt is dangerous. Not all debt is bad, and this is what confuses people.

Some forms of debt do you a world of good. Learning to distinguish between good and bad debt is one of the many crucial lessons you'll learn in this book.

Throughout this book, I've made it a point to keep the language as simple as possible so that you can quickly understand what I'm talking about. You don't need a degree in accounting or a special qualification to figure out what the deal is with your money.

What you need is the desire to understand your money fully and to get your finances in order. Even if you're good with money now, there's a lot you can learn from this book. For example, many people think they're in a good position because they have money invested in a savings account. While this is better than nothing, putting all of your money in a savings account isn't "investing" it.

If all of your money is tied up in a savings account, you're losing money every day. This is just one of the many insights you'll learn while reading this book. I must also mention that some of this advice is going to make you uncomfortable. You might realize you've been doing things incorrectly for a while, and you'll face many questions within yourself.

You might think that your friends and family advise you on one thing, but this book tells you something else. Everyone's natural inclination is to trust those around them the most. However, I can assure you that this book's advice is time tested and is the correct advice. Those around you may have received incorrect information so take the time to educate them as well.

The desire to improve and to achieve a goal is everything. As an athlete, you already know this. While you're used to pushing your mind and body beyond your physical limits, the time has come to tackle an issue that will become bigger later in your life. If you're relatively young right now, you might think you have much time to get your money in order. This is true, but it's the wrong mindset to adopt.

To successfully figure out your money and get it working for you, you need to develop a mindset that prioritizes your money and financial well-being. Without this present, no advice will solve your issues or help you tackle potential ones. So get excited about your money and the fact that you're taking action to figure it out! You're already ahead of most people in this world, not just athletes.

Most people do not have the courage or inclination to understand their finances. They'd rather sweep the problem under the carpet. This isn't you. So pat yourself on the back for taking a great first step! It's now time to move ahead and take another step.

CHAPTER 1

ASSETS AND LIABILITIES

The poor and the middle class work for money. The rich have money work for them.

—ROBERT KIYOSAKI

TO FULLY UNDERSTAND MONEY, you need first to figure out what the deal is with assets and liabilities. Here's a simple definition: Assets are things that give you something in return. This could be money, or it could be something such as a good feeling. For example, nutritional supplements can get expensive. However, they help your body recover faster and help you perform better on the field. Despite their high cost, they're assets.

A liability is an object that doesn't give you anything of value. For example, a fancy car is a huge liability. You need to pay an exorbitant amount to purchase it and maintain it. In return, what does it give you? A few cool pics on Instagram, and that's about it. You might get a few admiring looks when you pull up outside a fashionable spot. However, do you need to buy a car to receive these looks? Someone who pulls up in a rental behind you will receive the same looks, and they'll spend a lot less than you.

Many people get confused between assets and liabilities because they think of them as being objects. For example, a fancy car is a liability, and a house is an asset. This is the wrong way to think because a fancy car can become an asset, and a house can become a liability. To better understand the differences between assets and liabilities, we need to look at two important components of your finance equation.

These are cash flow and net worth. Let's tackle cash flow first.

CASH FLOW

Cash flow refers to the money you receive every month that allows you to pay your bills, save a certain amount, and invest the rest. Cash in hand is extremely important since you need it to live according to your lifestyle's demands. You pursue your goals on the field or court to generate enough cash to live well. This might not be your primary purpose, but without cash, it's close to impossible to live well. Would you be able to live according to your current situation if you weren't getting paid to do what you do?

There are two components to cash flow. The first is the amount of cash you receive or your cash inflow. The second is your cash outflow, which is the amount of cash you use to pay for your expenses. If your inflow is greater than your outflow, your cash on hand will increase. If it's the opposite, your cash on hand will decrease. The first lesson you need to learn is: Never spend more than your cash inflow.

Active and Passive

Following the principle to never spend more than your cash inflow, we can conclude that it's important for you to maximize it. The greater your cash inflow is, the more money you'll have to spend on the things that satisfy you. You'll have more money to invest and to give to those you care about. For most people, their primary source of cash inflow is their job.

As an athlete, you receive income from the fruits of what you do on your playing field. Your team or sponsor pays you a certain amount of money as a part of your contract. This is similar to a salary that regular folks receive when they work at a nine to five job. In exchange for their effort in the office (field) and their time, they receive compensation.

This source of cash is referred to as being active or time-bound. The amount of cash you receive is strongly linked with the time you spend achieving desired results. For example, your salary is tied to your performance on the field. If you could achieve elite performance without spending time working out, taking care of your mind and body, you would still get paid.

However, as every JV athlete knows, you need to train like the best to be the best. You cannot get away from spending time in practice if you want elite results. Thus, your salary is ultimately linked to the amount of time you spend preparing. Elite athletes, such as those in the NFL or the NBA, get paid millions to do what they love. However, they also spend their entire day training and hire staff to look after their needs. Their time is fully linked to the amount of money they earn.

Active sources of income are great because it's easy to figure out how you can increase the amount you receive from them. For example, you could train better or spend more time working on a skillset and boost your performance. Everyone needs to have an active source of income. The problem is that their nature limits active income sources.

Since they're linked to your time, there's only so much you can earn. You have just 24 hours per day to exchange for money. You need to sleep for at least 10 hours every day to rest and recover. This leaves you with 14 hours to exchange for money. Of these 14 hours, you need to spend at least four to five hours eating and spending time with your loved ones.

This leaves you with nine hours to exchange for money. Everyone's time is limited, and as a result, the income they earn from an active source is also limited. No matter how great your results are, your earnings are limited based on how much time you've spent producing them. If you find that you need to spend more time producing them, you'll have to cut back on other things in your life. You might have to spend 12 hours of training and spend just two hours with your loved ones and on nutrition.

Most people cannot make such sacrifices indefinitely. As an athlete, the number of years you can earn money by playing a sport is limited. There will always be someone younger, faster, and stronger. You can't fight time. Athletes that retire choose other sources of active income. They end up neglecting to develop the second type of cash flow in their lives.

Passive Income

Passive income is tougher to generate than active income, but it's far more rewarding. This type of cash inflow is disconnected from your time spent generating it. You'll need to put the time in upfront to develop the source, but once this is done, it goes away and keeps making you money. The more passive income you have, the greater is the degree of financial freedom in your life.

Imagine living a life where you receive a steady income every month without having to go to work. This is a life that a lot of retirees live, and it's fully possible for you as well. It takes planning and a good understanding of how important passive income is for your cash inflow. Let's say you're receiving a monthly salary of $7,000. This is a pretty good income. Now imagine if someone mailed you a check of $3,000 every month, no questions asked. You didn't have to do anything to produce that income. You simply received it.

That's what passive income is. It allows you to earn money while you sleep. If you have enough passive income, you can do whatever you like with your time and not have to worry about how you'll pay for your living expenses. Sounds great, doesn't it? The catch is that generating enough passive income to pay for your living expenses is tough. Almost every source of passive income involves investing money and earning interest or returns on it.

A savings bank account is a source of passive income. You invest money into it, and you earn around one percent or less as a return every year. Let's say you need to generate $7,000 every month to pay for your expenses and live comfortably. $7,000 per month is $84,000 per year. How much will you need to invest in a savings account to receive this much money every year?

Interest earned every year = Amount invested * interest rate.

Amount invested = Interest earned every year/interest rate = 84,000/0.01 = $8,400,000

You'll need to invest $8.4 million to earn $84,000 per year or $7,000 per month. That's a lot of money! There are other sources of passive income that pay you higher interest rates, but even the best of these will pay you around four to five percent every year. There are ways of boosting your cash return through the use of leverage.

Leverage in financial terms refers to borrowing money. Let's say you wanted to generate $7,000 per month as a passive income from a savings account. You know that you need $8.4 million. Let's say you had just $84,000 to invest (which is also a lot, but this is just an example). What if someone allowed you to borrow $8.4

million on the basis of investing $84,000? They're willing to let you keep $84,000 in interest income and only ask to be paid whatever excess you receive over that Amount every year.

Interest earned = Total investment * interest rate = $(8,400,000+84,000)*.01 = 8,484,000*.01 = \$84,840$

Your desired cash inflow = $84,000

Excess cash received from investment = $84,840 - 84,000 = \$840$

Rate of return on your investment = cash you received/ amount you invested = $84,000/84,000 = 100\%$

This is a pretty sweet deal. It also happens to be beyond unrealistic that anyone would be willing to lend you money like this. However, it goes to show the power of leverage. With $84,000, you can control $8,484,000, and you can turn a one percent interest payment into a 100% gain.

Real estate investments allow you to access leverage, but at far lower rates than the ones cited in the example above. In the above example, you paid $84,000 to control $8,484,000. The $84,000 is called your "equity" in the deal. Think of it as being your piece of the pie.

Equity percentage in a deal = (cash invested / total cash in the deal)*100 = $(84,000/8,484,000)*100 = 0.99\%$

In the above example, you own 0.99% of the overall pie. In a normal real estate deal, you'll own anywhere between three percent to 20% of the pie when starting out. In exchange for giving you money, a lender will charge you interest over a number of years. The lower your equity is, the higher your monthly payment will be.

A loan that is drawn against property is called a mortgage.

Mortgages are a perfect example of how debt can be good or bad, and I'll explain this later in this chapter. Let's look at why drawing a mortgage might be a good idea. You can use it to buy a property and place it on rent. Your tenants will pay you rent monthly, and this becomes a source of passive cash flow for you. You'll need to maintain the property and manage it well, but the Amount of money you earn from it isn't tied to the time you spend maintaining it. Carry out preventive maintenance once in a while, and you'll generate the same amount of cash every month.

Real estate investments are a great source of passive income, and this is why many investors flock to it. You will need to go into debt to finance the deal, but as long as you manage it well, this is not a bad thing. Other sources of passive cash flow are business investments. You could invest money in a business that someone else is running, and you could receive a yearly or monthly cash payment.

You could set up an online business that can be fully automated. This will bring you cash flow every month without you having to do anything beyond maintaining the automated processes. The stock market is another source of passive income. Typically, you can earn a return of three to five percent on your investments.

Many retirees use financial instruments called annuities to generate passive income. There are many different kinds of annuities, but all of them require you to invest a lump sum amount with an insurer or a financial firm. You'll receive a certain monthly payment depending on when you want the payments to start and for how long you want to be paid.

Don't get caught up with types of instruments. Understand the difference between passive cash flow and active cash flow. The more passive your cash flow is, the greater is your financial and time freedom. Since passive cash flow requires investment, this will bring you into touch with the second part of your personal finance equation. You've learned about cash flow, and now it's time to look at net worth.

NET WORTH

Rich people often talk in terms of net worth. For example, look at the Forbes billionaires list. You'll see that Jeff Bezos, the CEO of Amazon, is "worth" over $100 billion. If the stock market drops, you'll read about how Bezos had "$100 million wiped out" from his wealth. These kinds of proclamations are pure nonsense. This is because the writers of these publications have no clue how money works. Therefore, pay no heed to such sensationalist headlines.

The reason such statements are false is that they refer to Bezos' net worth. Your net worth is the sum of all your assets, minus your liabilities. If you have $100 in cash and $80 in debts, your net worth is $20 (100-80). This is a simple net worth calculation and is a good approximation of how much cash you truly have. However, the type of assets you have can complicate the calculation.

Let's say you own a property (fully paid off) worth $1 million. You have $100 cash in the bank as before and have a credit card debt of $10,000. Your net worth is:

Net worth = Assets - liabilities = Property value + cash - credit card debt = 1,000,000+100-10,000 = $990,100

This paints quite a rosy picture. You're worth close to a million dollars. However, is this a true representation of your cash position? You have just $100 in the bank but are carrying debt worth $10,000. How are you going to pay this bill when it comes due? You can't sell a chunk of your property and use that to pay your bill. Properties don't work like that. Selling a million dollar property to pay a $10,000 credit card bill doesn't seem to be the right thing to do either.

After all, your property could increase in value. It could be worth $2,000,000 in a few years. This example shows how easy it is to get caught up in your net worth and why net worth calculations matter only to a certain point. It would help if you had the cash flow to pay for your living expenses. If you don't have this, it doesn't matter what your net worth is.

What if you have enough cash flow to pay your bills and set aside enough for an emergency but have a low net worth? Is that desirable? Let's say you earn $7,000 per month, which covers all expenses and leaves you with $4,000 in savings, which you put into a bank account that pays you interest. You don't own property or any kinds of physical assets. Is this a good situation?

While it's much better than the previous situation,

it's still not ideal. It would help if you balanced your net worth considerations with your cash flow. Take care of your cash flow above everything else and invest the rest into building assets that boost your net worth. You'll learn how to spot such assets shortly.

A great example of how you can think about net worth versus cash flow comes from the billionaire Warren Buffett. Buffett has been in the top five of Forbes' list since the late 1990s. His net worth has hovered north of $50 billion since that time. Despite this astronomical net worth, he draws a yearly salary of $100,000 from his company. That's how much he needs to pay his bills and have peace of mind regarding cash flow.

As far as Buffett is concerned, the majority of his net worth is just a scorecard. He's an investor, so he uses it to keep tabs on how good his investment decisions are. In terms of paying bills and paying for his daily needs, he couldn't care less about his net worth. Your net worth is important to the extent to which it brings you peace of mind. Let's look at another example that will illustrate the difference.

Let's say you have $1 million in the bank as cash. Another person owns a $1 million property they can live in and has zero cash. Who is better off? The person with cash is. The person with the property still needs to pay bills and maintenance. They have a high net worth but of what use is it? You can't eat a house. Let's now change this up a bit.

The second person now owns the $1 million property and has $500,000 in the bank that they're using to generate passive income to the tune of five percent every year. This means they earn (0.05*500,000) $25,000 every year which is $2,083 every month. What's more, they've placed the $1 million home on rent and are earning $9,000 per month from their tenants.

Their monthly cash flow is (9,000+2,083) $11,083. Over and above this, they work a full-time job, which pays them $8,000 per month. This brings their overall cash inflow to $19,083. Their expenses are $5,000 per month, which leaves them with a final cash flow of $14,083. They're now using this money to build a business that will bring them even more cash flow.

Compare all of this to the person who has just $1 million in the bank and is doing nothing with it. Who is better off? The second person is. This example illustrates a basic fact about money. Money is worth something only when it's "flowing" from one source to another. It's best if it flows into something that produces more of it instead of flowing into a liability. This is where the first rule of money will help you. Never spend more than your cash inflow, and you'll not have to worry about running out of cash.

Your cash flow can be used to build your net worth, but your net worth is just a scorecard. It doesn't mean anything tangible unless you're using it to generate more cash. This doesn't mean you neglect net worth. It's just that net worth is a result of how well you use your cash. Don't get caught up in net worth calculations and mistake this for wealth. It's paper money. If the stock market falls and Jeff Bezos' net worth dips by $100 million, he isn't losing cash. His paper money has reduced, and he probably doesn't care about it.

Falling into the net worth trap is common amongst many real estate investors. This is because they don't understand what assets and liabilities are.

ASSETS AND LIABILITIES

How many times have you heard of someone brag about their million-dollar property portfolio or "empire?" Have you read online ads that present some spotty 16-year-old kid as being a property millionaire? I'm highlighting real estate because it's a great example of how misunderstood leverage is. It also highlights how the lines between assets and liabilities can blur into a hot mess if you don't take the time to understand them properly.

Let's begin by defining what an asset is. An asset is something that increases your cash inflow. This deceptively simple definition will save you from a world of pain. Some people think of assets as being investments that increase their net worth. This is false and is a great way of falling into debt traps. Always look at assets as investments that increase your cash inflow. We're not done defining an asset yet.

The second quality an asset must have is maintaining itself and not putting you at risk of falling into a debt hole that will wipe you out. Let's analyze a few investment opportunities to see whether they qualify as assets. The first example is that of a real estate investment.

The property is worth $500,000, and you need to

borrow money to buy it. Let's say your equity in the deal is 20%. This means you invest $100,000 and borrow $400,000 from a bank. They ask you to pay a certain amount of cash every month for the next 30 years. Let's assume this monthly payment is $300. You earn $4,000 every month from your job. With me so far? Great!

Your net worth = Assets - liabilities = Property equity - Debt owed = 100,000-400,000 = -$300,000

Monthly cash flow = Cash inflow - cash outflow = 4,000- 300 = $3,700

You now have a choice as to how you want to use this property. You could do what most people do and live in it. This advice is quite common and is presented as being a way to "pay yourself." Are you paying yourself, however? Once you live in this house, your net worth remains the same. However, your cash outflow increases because you'll have to pay for maintenance, utilities, and more. Let's say this amount is $2,000 per month.

Net worth = -$300,000

Monthly cash flow = Cash inflow - cash outflow = 4,000 - (300+2,000) = $1,700

Is this investment an asset? Going back to our two rules for an asset, it doesn't increase your cash inflow. It doesn't pay for itself, and it's put you in a debt hole of $400,000. This debt costs you just $300 per month, which is a very small portion of your monthly cash inflow. However, what happens if you lose your job? How will you pay the mortgage then? Stop making payments, and the bank will foreclose on it, and you'll be out on the street. This house is not an investment.

You can turn it into an investment, however. You decide to place the property on rent and earn $5,000 per month in rent. You'll need to live in a rental property, which costs $2,000 per month, which adds to your cash outflow. What does the equation look like now?

Net worth = -$300,000

Monthly cash flow = Cash inflow - cash outflow = (Salary earned + Rental amount earned) - (Mortgage payment + Rent paid + Maintenance expenses) = (4,000+5,000) - (300+2,000+2,000) = $4,700

Before you bought this property, your cash inflow was equal to your salary, which was $4,000. The property has created expenses, but it's increased your monthly cash flow by $700. It ticks the first box to qualify as an asset. You need to spend $2,000 on monthly rent to live and another $2,000 on maintaining the property, over and above the mortgage expense. This is paid for by the rental money you earn every month. If you were to lose your job, it's not going to put you in a massive debt hold because the rental payment covers all expenses related to the property. It ticks the second box as well. This is a great asset.

As you can see, the same property can behave as an asset or as a liability. If you haven't caught on as yet, a liability is the opposite of an asset. It decreases your monthly cash flow, and it puts you in a debt hole. You turned a liability into an asset by placing the house on rent and deciding to rent your own living space. Can you see why the notion of "paying yourself first" is incorrect? Can you see the number of details that it misses?

I'm not saying it's better to rent versus buy. My point is that you need to calculate your net worth (to figure out your overall debt), your monthly cash flow (to figure out cash inflows versus outflows), and use this to arrive at a full picture.

I'd also like to point out an error that real estate investors fall into. The property in our example was worth $500,000. Many investors assume that just because they control a property worth this amount, they're now worth that much. This is completely false. As long as you have an outstanding mortgage, you don't own anything. You only own equity in the property. This is why the net worth figure is negative.

This isn't a problem, however. If the property is an asset, the rental amount is paying for every expense related to it, so you don't need to worry about falling into a debt hole. As long as you have tenants, you can finance your mortgage, and you won't have to worry about foreclosure.

Contrast this with a real estate "emperor" who claims to be worth $1 million. What they have is $200,000 in equity and $800,000 in mortgages. Their properties might be paid for by the rent, which is great. However, what if the economy tanks and they stop earning rental payments? They're now in a debt hole because they bought too many properties using debt. Bankruptcy is their only option. So much for being "worth" a million.

In the example, we just looked at, what happens if you stop earning rental income on your property? You still have your full-time job ($4,000), allowing you to pay the mortgage ($300). You can still afford to pay your own rental expense ($2,000). Maintenance ($2,000) takes a hit, but you can hopefully keep things at a minimum standard until your next tenant arrives. You're not going to fall into a debt hole or have to declare bankruptcy.

You can use leverage (debt) to boost your net worth, but the more you use, the greater is your risk. As long as you understand that risk and have plans to counter it, you can create an asset. Don't do this, and you'll be creating liability and will require luck to be successful. It's far better to rely on processes and skills instead of luck to be successful. As an athlete, you already know this.

Another Case Study

We've looked at real estate, what about the stock market? The stock market is the other major investment area, so it's worth looking at an example to see whether an investment here is truly an asset. Most stock market investments prioritize net worth boosts over cash flow. Let's say you've invested $10,000 into the market, and this pays you no cash. Its value fluctuates up or down, and that's it.

Since this investment doesn't generate cash inflows, you might be tempted to classify it as a liability (as per the previously stated rules). However, this is not true. You can always sell the investment down the road for a higher price, increasing your cash inflow. Your net worth will be boosted along the way, through the paper gains that your investment realizes.

As far as monthly cash flow is concerned, as long as you're investing money that you can afford, your cash flow isn't impacted. If you're earning $4,000 per month and can invest $1,000 safely, your cash flow isn't impacted negatively. You don't need to spend cash on maintaining the investment; it goes away and behaves as it will. Therefore, this is an asset.

I must point out that a key criterion for something to qualify as an asset is to understand how it works. If you don't understand how it works, you're not creating an asset. I'll explain how to understand best the stock market and real estate investments later in the book. For now, you need to understand what assets and liabilities are.

Can you see why a fancy car is now a liability? It costs you money every month and puts you in a debt hole. How can you turn this into an asset? What if you could lease it to someone to drive for Uber? You'll earn some cash on it, and this reduces your debt burden. You could use it for advertising brands and earning sponsor cash. This will probably allow you to drive it for free (since the sponsor cash will be greater than the monthly payment).

There is a qualitative aspect to an asset you must consider. If you need a vehicle to perform your job well, it's not necessarily a liability. In such cases, you should minimize the negative cash impact. For example, instead of buying a fancy new car, buy an old one for cash. This way, you're not creating a debt burden beyond what is strictly necessary.

Take some time now to think of various examples in your own life. Look at the objects you already own and analyze whether they're assets or liabilities. Is your wallet a liability? How about your clothes? At which point does shopping for expensive clothes go from being an asset to a liability? How about shoes? Watches?

Examine everything. This will train you to think in terms of assets and liabilities. Most importantly, look at your time as an asset. How are you spending it? Spend it training or on the field, and it's an asset. Spend it with people who drag you down and leech off you, and it's a liability. You don't need to be hardcore and train all the time. Relaxation and entertainment are important, as well. However, realize that too much of something can turn an asset into a liability. Everything is a tool, and it's up to you to create assets as much as possible.

CHAPTER 2

MANAGING CASH FLOW

Never take your eyes off the cash flow because it's the life blood of business.

—RICHARD BRANSON

CASH FLOW IS IMPORTANT, and managing it is crucial for your financial situation to remain in a happy place. Managing your cash flow is a tough skill to master. Everyone wants to enjoy the fruits of their labor, so it's natural to want to spend cash on the things you enjoy. If you have someone close to you who needs some cash, it's normal to want to be able to help them out.

Managing cash flow requires some mental skills, as well as some clerical ones. It would help if you looked at the things you want to spend your cash on in the right manner. I'm not saying you need to cut out all forms of enjoyment from your life. Some people think that managing their money means they need to stop having fun. Instead, it would help if you looked at financial discipline as a means of gaining financial freedom.

Without the discipline to practice every day, you cannot be successful on the field. Similarly, without the discipline to manage your money, you cannot hope to get it to work for you. Think of your money as being your best employee. Put this employee to work as much as possible since they'll never tire of it. In fact, not putting it to work is what tires money out.

It would be easy for me to give you a list of budgeting tools and teach you how to manage cash flow, but the fact is that you need to get your head right first. Everything begins with the mind, as you already know. Let's take some time to examine the beliefs and thoughts you have around money.

YOUR MONEY FRAMEWORK

What do you think when you think about money? You've read stories of athletes that earned millions during their playing careers but ended up broke, having to declare bankruptcy. Examples such as LeBron James seem to be rare. James never went to college and earned millions right out of high school. However, he's never been involved in any financial scandal and has never had issues with money throughout his illustrious career. How does he manage it?

While James's specific techniques are unknown,

there's no doubt that his mindset regarding money is airtight. He views it as a resource and does not spend it frivolously. While he does buy himself luxuries, he doesn't throw his money away on bad investments or people who aren't worth his time.

James' success with money is proof that it's far more important to possess the right mindset regarding money than it is to receive some special education. It also proves that no matter one's background, it's possible to develop this mindset. James grew up in inner-city poverty and without a father (Kozlowski, 2020). He was thrust into the national spotlight during his freshman year in high school, and despite all of that, he's managed to make his money work for him.

What are some of your beliefs surrounding money?

Money is Bad/Difficult to Make/Evil

Money is a necessary part of our lives, and it happens to be an intensely emotional topic. We learn a lot about money from those around us when we're young. How our parents and caregivers treated money and thought about it defines our deeply embedded beliefs about it. If you grew up in a religious household, you might have heard all about how money corrupts and so on.

We're the product of our innermost beliefs. Is it plausible to think you'd be good at managing money if you believed it was evil? This would be impossible. It's like thinking you're terrible at your sport and still trying to be successful. You can train all you want, but if you don't believe it, you're not going to succeed.

If you spot this particular belief within you, recognize

what a huge hurdle it is, and resolve to remove it from your mind. The best way to do this is to install a new belief and to remind yourself of it at all times. Examine how money helps you live a better life. Notice that everything around you comes from the existence of money. How would people eat food without money? How can beautiful buildings and works of art be created without money?

Money is just a tool that allows people to express themselves more freely. If someone used a knife to harm someone, would you turn around and say it was the knife's fault? Money is no more at fault than your shoes are when it comes to creating misfortune or corruption. It's a tool that can be used for good or bad. Use it for good, and it will bring untold prosperity into your life. Use it poorly, and you'll only create harm in your life.

Money Should be Used to...

People have different opinions about what money should be used for. Some people associate money with enjoyment and spend it all on things that bring them the most joy. Others see it as a source of trouble and end up minimizing their spending and don't deal with their money in healthy and financially lucrative ways.

The key is to develop a balance between these viewpoints. While money can be used to bring joy into your life, you need to use it for necessities. As an athlete, your prime is limited, and if you want to maximize your best years, you need to learn how money ought to be used. The answer is quite simple.

The majority of your money should be used to build

assets. It's impossible to avoid spending money on liabilities, so it's best to minimize such spending. Do not spend money on liability until you've spent twice that amount on an asset. For example, if you want to spend money buying a fancy watch, have you spent twice that amount on an asset first? Only buy the watch once you've done this.

Awareness of your spending habits is crucial. Look back at your expenses over the past month and make a list of everything that you bought. How many of these were necessities? How many were wants? Wants are the things that you don't strictly need to survive. You need clothes to survive, but do you need that sparkling Armani suit? Ask yourself, why did you buy those things, and what was their utility?

An object's utility goes beyond what you used it for. Did it make you feel good? How long did this feeling last? A house that you've had your eye on for 20 years is going to leave a deeper impression on you than a fancy suit that you saw in passing and felt like buying. The greater the utility of the things you buy, the better your spending is.

Check to see if you're using money to cover up some other perceived shortcomings in your life. People often do this, and it's a great way to convince yourself that money is the root of all evil. This happens because no number of purchases can help you overcome feelings of inadequacy. The more money you spend, the worse you'll feel, and the logical conclusion at that point will be to say that money is what's causing you problems. In reality, it's your unwillingness, to be honest with yourself; that's the issue.

Try to make a list of all the things you believe to be true about money and create positive statements to counter them. For example, if you think you cannot learn how to manage your money, tell yourself that managing money is a skill and that any skill can be learned with enough practice. Read these positive beliefs to yourself every morning once you wake up, and once before you go to bed. Remind yourself of them during every waking moment.

BUDGETING

As you start installing positive beliefs around money within yourself, you'll find that the task of budgeting and tracking your expenses becomes a lot easier. If you've never budgeted in your life before this, it's going to be tough. It's a lot like learning to ride a bike. You're going to fall a few times, but once you're done falling, you're unlikely to forget how to do it.

Once you get good with budgeting and tracking your expenses, you'll likely not even need to formally track your spending since you'll develop a feel for how much money you're spending and will spend your cash accordingly. Budgeting is a task that is often mishandled because of how people view it. Budgets are viewed as tools that curtail an individual's freedom. As I mentioned earlier, it's best for you to realize that financial discipline is what sets you free.

A key question that often arises when budgeting is, how should you allocate your money? The best answer to this is to utilize the 50/30/20 budget.

50/30/20

This budget was popularized by Senator Elizabeth Warren and her daughter (Yates, 2017). The premise is quite simple. You spend 50% of your money on your expenses (needs). You spend 30% on wants, and the remaining 20% is placed as savings. The simplicity of this method is what makes it powerful.

Your needs are the things that you have to have to survive and do what you do. Food expenses, transportation, rent, insurance, and basic entertainment are examples of needs. Entertainment might be a head-scratcher. It's hard for most people to view a night out on the town as a "need," even if they'd love to indulge in it.

There's no need for you to cut out your entertainment expenses completely. This is unrealistic and will be detrimental to your mental health. Instead, learn where you need to draw a line. Much like the previous example with clothes, you need some degree of entertainment. You don't need to go around buying everyone drinks at the bar. You don't need to throw lavish parties for those around you. If someone expects you to do this for them because you have money, then it's probably time to cut that person out of your life.

Your wants are the things that bring you happiness in the short term. For example, you could spot a nice pair of shoes that you would like to own. Another example might be buying fancy clothes or a car. Wants feel great, but the satisfaction they bring usually dissipates after a short while. Once the new car smell subsides, you're left with a vehicle that guzzles gas and needs constant maintenance.

Many people end up blowing their money on wants, which is why the 50/30/20 framework is powerful. It gives you clear instructions on how to spend your money. When creating your budget, list all of your needs separately, and list your wants as a single line item. You can even call it "wants." Record all of these expenses here. This will help reinforce that wants are not necessary and that it doesn't matter what the individual item is. As long as it's a want, it isn't all that important.

Lastly, we have investments, which you'll allocate 20% of your income towards. The original framework, as proposed by Senator Warren, includes debt repayment in this category, but this isn't the best way to use your money. Debt repayment is not investing any more than eating medicine for an ailment is one. Much like how the problem with the latter situation is an underlying disease, debt is a problem. Repaying it isn't investing your money in anything. If you had a disease, you'd spare no expense getting rid of it. Your approach to debt should be similar. I'll address this shortly.

Investments include money placed in stocks, real estate, and other assets. Savings accounts are not technically assets, and you'll learn why later in this book. It's always prudent to invest your money in places where it can grow. This is simply putting money to work and to increase the speed with which it flows in your life.

While 50/30/20 is a great way to simplify your

spending allocations, it isn't necessary for you to follow these exact proportions. Leaving the world of athletes aside, many people who end up prosperous usually spend less than 40% of their incomes on living expenses. This includes expenditures that can be classified as wants.

This leaves them with 60% of their incomes as savings, and they deploy this money to create more passive income for themselves. Allocating just 20% of your income to savings and investments might work if your income is low. However, as your income increases, it's a good idea to increase that proportion and reduce your spending on wants and needs as much as realistically possible.

The true purpose of investment is to create passive income and assets. You've learned in the previous chapter that doing this takes time and much money. Therefore, it makes sense for you to invest as much as possible, as quickly as possible. You'll learn more about this in the chapter on investment.

Monitor your spending for a month and decide on which proportion makes sense for you. Remember to classify your needs and wants correctly. No one is asking you to give up on your wants. Instead, decrease your degree of spending on them. For example, many people tend to overdo their cheat meals. The correct way to implement a cheat meal is to reduce the amount of food you eat in those meals. Instead of eating an entire pizza, have just a slice. Instead of eating an entire sundae, with Nutella heaped on top, have a scoop of ice cream.

Similarly, don't spend large amounts of money on

your wants. Aim to reduce those expenditures by 10% until you can go no lower. If you eat out a lot (no matter how healthy the food might be), cut down this expense by 10% every month. If you spend $200 eating out, aim to spend $180, then $162, and so on. Eventually, you'll reach a stage you'll find it hard to go lower than. This is your optimal level. Awareness and tracking are key.

Tracking Methods

There are two broad ways to track your spending. The first is to track everything in a spreadsheet manually. The second is to use an app. You probably track your calories already in one form or another, so view this as just being an extension of this practice. Manual tracking is straightforward, but it requires you to devote time to performing clerical work.

You'll need to save all of your receipts and enter them accordingly. You'll have to create a pivot table in Excel and track your spending in various categories. Apps make this part of the process easier, but you'll have to spend time classifying expenses. Many apps connect to your bank account and pull expenditures from there directly. As a result, a fancy meal will be categorized as part of your grocery expenses instead of going under entertainment or as a want.

Apps allow you to create your categories, but they don't always support tracking to the most minute detail level. For example, aim to track food expenses by dividing expenses between proteins, carbs, and fat (or rice, protein sources, vegetables, and fat). An app can't do this automatically. It can help you track items only down to the receipt level. You'll need to buy these things separately to automate that level of tracking.

As a result, if you're interested in granular tracking, a manual method works best. If this isn't a concern, use an app. Mint is the best app for financial tracking. It's the oldest app on the market and connects to your bank accounts easily. It also pulls credit card spending and provides reminders for bill payments. There are other apps such as YNAB and Toshl Finance, but Mint is probably the best.

YNAB (You Need A Budget) is best for those carrying a significant amount of debt that needs to be paid off. You'll learn how to approach the question of debt reduction in the next chapter. Make it a habit to start tracking your expenses according to your preferred tracking method. Whatever method you choose, you'll need to spend some time collecting all data together and analyzing it.

Mint provides an easy to understand pie chart that classifies spending according to your categories. You can fix spending limits on each line item, or you can fix an overall limit to your needs, wants, and investments according to your proportion. Fixing an overall limit is probably the better option since some of your line item expenses might spill over. If you wish to go down the line item route, here are the most common expenses you'll have:

- Rent/living costs
- Gym/fitness costs

- Transportation
- Health insurance
- Car insurance (if applicable)
- Food and supplements
- Entertainment
- Cost of support services (mental health, physical recovery etc.)
- Phone and internet
- Utilities
- Grooming
- Miscellaneous
- Education

The most important items on this list are the last two. Miscellaneous expenses give you a bucket to classify expenses that don't fit a particular line item. They also give you a buffer. You may over or underestimate some of your expenses. A bucket that can catch any spills is essential in a budget.

Education in this context refers to investing in yourself. You invest in your body by exercising and training, but how much are you investing in your mind? The easiest way to invest in your mind is to read. Books are the best investments you can make. With the rise of eBooks, you can pay a few dollars to buy great books. Through programs such as Amazon's Kindle, you can rent books for a while without having to pay the full price for the book.

Your playing days won't last forever, so you need to start preparing yourself as early as possible. It's easy to think that you'll always be invincible when you're in your prime, but this is not the case. If you were lucky enough to graduate with a degree, continue to invest in that education. If not, work towards attaining some form of education. It doesn't have to be a college degree. Learn real-world skills such as managing your money (this book is an investment in your education) or programming.

Whichever skill catches your fancy, set aside some time to learn what it takes to develop that skill. You don't need to master it overnight. Perhaps you'd like to start a business after your career is finished. Spend some time networking with people who can show you the ropes. Perhaps one of your sponsors can teach you this? Get creative and aim to educate yourself. Doing this alone will prevent you from falling into a debt trap or going bankrupt later in life.

Invest in courses that enhance your skills. If you want to learn about real estate investing, you could either pay a successful investor for their time to teach you some of the ropes, or you could take a course online. Suppose computers have fascinated you, but you've never had the time to learn to program. In that case, you can learn online or attend a coding boot camp during your offseason.

A great and free educational resource is YouTube. Every skill on the planet is covered via a YouTube video these days. While you can't learn everything from these videos, you can learn a lot about a topic. You can take various topics out for a test drive before committing to one subject. Doing this goes back to my point in the previous chapter about investing your time. The thing about investing is that all the benefits it gives you compounds. One benefit builds on top of another until the progress you make outstrips the sum of the individual benefits.

Commit to spending at least one hour daily to educating yourself. If you're busy, this is much time. However, find a way to do this. You could watch videos during your meals, or you could spend some time with someone who has the skills you want. Over time, you'll end up building a large body of knowledge that will stand you in good stead.

Take some time right now to figure out how you want to create your budget. What are the line items that apply to you, and how will you track all of them? How will you invest your time, and which metrics can you use to track this? You could measure the results of this time by reviewing the new skills you've learned or viewing how well you're performing certain actions. It's entirely up to you.

What's important is that you take what you've learned in this and the previous chapter and start applying it. Remember the lessons about assets and liabilities? Is the time spent creating a budget and tracking it an asset or a liability? When you need to evaluate your needs versus wants, can you identify wants by viewing them through the perspective of assets and liabilities? Spend some time thinking about all of this, and creating a budget to manage your cash flow will become easy.

CHAPTER 3

DEBT

Some debts are fun when you are acquiring them, but none are fun when you set about retiring them.

—OGDEN NASH

WHAT IS the easiest way to go broke? Simple! Spend more than what you make and use your credit card to pay for your expenses. While you're at it, borrow money to buy liabilities. As you can see, there's not much that you need to do to push your financial position so deep in a hole that you'll never recover. So what should you do to avoid this situation? That's simple as well!

Avoid doing all of these negatives. Don't spend more than what you earn. Don't use credit cards to pay for your expenses (or use them sparingly and pay them off in full when the bill comes due) and don't borrow money to create a liability. Two of these things involve the use of debt. Credit cards charge you high-interest fees when you don't pay off your balance in full. Debt used to create liabilities was spotlighted in the first chapter when you learned how to evaluate what an asset truly is.

When you're out on the field, do you adopt a warrior-like mindset? Do you vow to conquer all your obstacles and give it your best, no matter what? This is pretty much the mindset you need to adopt when it comes to debt. Try to make no mistake; debt that pays for liabilities will make it impossible for you ever to be free. Debt is such a serious issue that I will tell you to ignore the 50/30/20 partition that I spoke about in the previous chapter.

In its place, you'll need to use another framework that will help you get rid of your debt as quickly as possible.

GETTING RID OF DEBT

The advice to ditch the 50/30/20 framework applies to you if you're currently carrying any form of debt. This could be student loan debt, vehicle-related debt, or credit card debt. Mortgages are a tricky subject, and I'll address these shortly. The other kinds of debt you owe have no reason to exist. Student loan debt especially makes no sense, so it's in your best interest to get rid of it as quickly as possible.

Many athletes carry high credit card debt levels because they tend to overspend the minute they start earning money. Your credit card is not a source of free money. Credit cards charge high levels of interest, and if you keep borrowing money at those rates, you're certain to go broke. Vehicle loans are a seemingly normal form of debt to assume, but they don't make any sense once again.

A vehicle's value reduces by up to 25% the minute you leave the dealer's lot. This applies to new cars and used cars, with the latter's values reducing to a lesser degree. A car's value only reduces over time (unless it happens to be a classic, in which case you can't drive it for everyday purposes). Drawing a loan to pay a car is like borrowing money to pay for a restaurant meal. Your food will go bad at some point, so why would you pay the cost of that meal back over a few years?

If you have an outstanding car loan, figure out the remaining amount you owe on it and start planning to save that money up. While you're at it, try to make a list of all the debts you have and order them from the highest interest rate to the lowest. Once this is done, you need to figure out how you will pay off the highest interest debt first.

We don't realize how damaging interest is for our finances. For example, if you use a loan to buy a car that sells for $20,000, at 4.6% interest over a period of five years, you'll pay $365 every month. This is a small amount and easily fits most budgets. However, over the course of five years, you're going to pay $22,020. This is 10% more than what the car sells for. The damage doesn't end there.

Your car's value is going to reduce (depreciate) over that period. It's going to be worth half of what it sold initially at the end of five years. It'll be worth around $10,000 in five years, and you'll pay $22,020 for something that is going to be worth $10,000. Would you give someone two dollars and receive $1 back in return? Of course, you wouldn't. Yet, this is what you're doing when you borrow money to finance a car.

You could turn this equation in your favor by turning your car into an asset. However, if you don't do that, it's one of the worst liabilities you can assume. This example highlights a $20,000 purchase. How much do you think you'd lose buying a Ferrari or another pasta rocket like the big ballers do? Those cars depreciate in the same manner as rock sinks in water. You'll also have to pay maintenance costs, which will be pretty high, close to 10% of the car's sticker price every year.

If you feel the need to drive a fancy car, do the smart thing and get yourself a sponsorship. You'll get paid to drive them around. If you can't land a deal, rent them for a few days, thrash them around, and return them to the rental company. That is what all these cars are good for. Don't be seduced by the pictures of fancy cars.

There are some other purchases that athletes purchase using debt. I'll highlight these for cautionary purposes at the end of this chapter. For now, let's look at how you're going to get rid of debt.

Financial Freedom

The first step to financial freedom is to get rid of debt. This means you need to reduce your spending on your wants to its bare bones. You need to carefully evaluate your needs and reduce your spending on them as much as possible. Even if it means living in situations that aren't quite up to your standard (as long as it's safe), you need to do this. You cannot save or grow your money as long as you have debt.

Pay your highest interest-bearing debt off first. This debt costs you the most, so pay down its principal instead of just making interest payments. Your monthly debt payments have two components: Principal and interest. Principal refers to the amount of money you've borrowed, and interest is the lender's profit. If you pay just the interest and not the principal, you're not making any progress with your debt.

Let's take credit cards as an example. You must have noticed by now that when the payment date comes closer, card companies highlight the minimum payment due? This amount is lesser than the overall balance. The minimum payment is presented as an easy solution for you. Pay far lesser than the amount you owe, and you can keep using your credit card. This is a trick that lenders and banks use to milk you dry.

The minimum payment that is due is just the interest on the amount you owe (the principal). Paying this amount does nothing to reduce your debt. You need to pay off as much of your balance as possible, as quickly as possible. Once you've paid off these balances, cut your credit cards up, and restrict yourself to making just one purchase every month on a card. Pay that off as soon as you get home.

The majority of the money you make must be dedicated to paying down your debt. It makes no sense to save money or invest the money as long as you're carrying debt. The money you save, let's say in a savings account, or even in a stock market investment that grows by eight percent every year, cannot compensate you for the interest you're paying. Your savings are growing at eight percent, but you've borrowed money at 22%. How can you ever expect to make money? 22% is the usual interest rate that credit card companies charge you.

So ignore all the advice about investing for as long as you're carrying debt. Get rid of debt first and then focus on investing in other ventures. If your debt burden is high, consider consolidating all of it into a few payments. You can use the services of debt consolidation advisors. If you have multiple credit lines through credit cards, transfer all of your outstanding debt onto a single card with the lowest interest rate.

Mortgages are the heftiest form of debt you can assume. They last for 30 years, so their ill-effects persist well after your playing days have ended. If you've created a liability using a mortgage, you need to figure out how to extricate yourself from it. Can you place the home on rent? Can you sell the place for a modest profit and get rid of your mortgage debt? Once you sell it, you can buy another property that you can rent and earn cash flow from.

Your property is an asset only if the rental payments cover the costs required to maintain it and the mortgage payment. If you're paying any money out of pocket, then this isn't an asset. If you wish to buy a house for a family member or a loved one, buy it in cash. Don't finance the purchase. If you cannot make payments down the road, not only will you suffer, the person you bought the home will lose as well.

Use an app such as YNAB to track your debt expenses and payments. Pay your principal amounts off as quickly as possible. This makes a huge difference to your monthly interest payments. The lower your principal is, the more your interest payments decrease. Add your debt repayment amount as a line item in your budget and make it a point to pay it every month. It comes before everything except rent/living expenses, food, and water. Minimize your wants and make debt repayment your top priority.

If you find it tough to stay the course, then remind yourself of the mindset you need to possess. I explained this at the start of this chapter. I'm not asking you to cut out entertainment expenses entirely. This would simply be punishing yourself, and that doesn't help anyone. Instead, minimize it. Instead of watching a movie in a theatre, can you watch it at home instead? This doesn't mean you load up on Netflix subscriptions. It means you find cheaper ways of entertainment. You're in no position to drop five figures at the club every night, so don't put yourself in such places.

Once you've paid your way out of debt, you need to focus on staying out of it.

STAYING OUT OF DEBT

The best way to stay out of debt is, to be honest with yourself. Are you bad with money, and do you struggle with monitoring your spending? If yes, then lean on someone close to you who can help you manage your finances. Do not outsource financial management to someone else under any circumstances. It's your money, and you should manage it. Lean on them for support and for timely reminders. You're still responsible for your behavior. It's not their job to spend your money for you. They're only present for support.

Switch to the 50/30/20 budget to give your spending a good framework. Your priority, once you've got rid of debt, is to establish a freedom fund. A freedom fund is the same as a rainy day fund, except its purpose is to make you financially free. If you save for rainy days, that's all you'll receive. Save for freedom, and that's what you'll get. This fund should have money equal to six months' to a year's worth of living expenditures.

You must place this money in a savings account to be easily accessible if things go bad for you. Having this money in the bank gives you much freedom since you can accept more investment opportunities and grow your money. You can experiment with different assets thanks to having this amount of money stashed away.

Once this fund is set up, you need to invest in real estate or the stock market. When investing in real estate, remember that you need to create an asset, not a liability. I'll cover investments in more detail in the next chapter.

Private investments, such as a friend's venture, also comes under this category. As you focus on building your financial framework, remember these tips to ensure you stay out of debt.

Recognize Your Window

As an athlete, your earning window is a fraction of the size of a regular person's. A person who works at an office can retain their position for close to 30 or 40 years. The average athlete has a window of 10 years, less in the case of physically demanding sports. The money you make in 10 years needs to last you for close to 50 years. In a regular person, they need to make money they earn over 40 years last for 20 to 30.

Given this reality, you need to make good financial decisions. Try not to rush into any decision without understanding everything about it. Don't get swept in the rush of having to grow your money as quickly as possible. Instead, follow the framework you've learned and keep stashing your money away for your future.

Educate Yourself

Your financial education doesn't end with this book. This is just the beginning. Make it a point to study finance and money as much as possible. Remember your education fund? That's what this is for. Read books and listen to people who know what they're talking about. Unless your childhood friend has a financial degree or has made much money by themselves, try not to listen to them.

Learn how to invest wisely. The next chapter's material is a good starting point but doesn't think that you're done once you read it. Education is a continuous process, and the more you learn, the better off you'll be. You'll have many people tugging at your wallet, so you need the education to protect you from losing all of your money.

Rein in Your Spending

Why do athletes go broke? Examine the case of pretty much any former athlete, and you'll see that all of them end up spending money on things that make no sense. For example, Allen Iverson, who earned more than $200 million during his time in the NBA, was forced to file bankruptcy because he couldn't pay an $860,000 bill for jewelry. There are two remarkable stats here. First, Iverson could not pay a bill that was just 0.43% of his total career earnings.

Second, he was spending six figures on jewelry despite knowing he could not pay the bill. He might not have known the extent of his poverty, but he certainly must have known that his money was running out. Jewelry is a particularly problematic expense since many people have false conceptions of it. I'll explain why this is at the end of this chapter when I list the worst purchases you can make with debt (or with cash).

If you feel the need to rock some bling, remember that it's better to be rich than to look rich. Have you ever seen Bill Gates wear any bling or even drive a fancy car? Gates is what real wealth looks like. The average rapper rocking his bling is what "broke in 10 years" looks like. Decide whom you want to be.

Keep Good Company

What's the best way to stay out of trouble? The

answer's obvious: don't go anywhere near it. Much like how Alcoholics Anonymous members stay away from bars and places that serve alcohol, you need to stay away from people and places that could potentially spell trouble. LeBron James might come across as extremely self-absorbed, but when have you ever read stories of him being in the middle of trouble at a club or having to appear in court because he was an accomplice to illegal activity?

I've already highlighted James' tough upbringing, so it's not a question of growing up in the wrong neighborhood. All that matters are your priorities. If you choose to stick with people who constantly get into and out of trouble, it's a matter of time before you're going to get dragged into it. Keep your circle close, and do not let anyone manipulate you into spending your money.

If you're unsure of whether you're spending your money the right way, use professional help and seek their advice. Going back to LeBron James' example, you might look at how he hired his friends to manage and build his empire. However, his manager and close friend Maverick Carter has always said that it wasn't about giving friends and family a free ride. Everyone on the team had to bring skills to the table. Without it, there was no point in giving them access to James' money.

Cater has also spoken about how James and his team used the example of Jay-Z as a model of wealth-building (Rhoden, 2018). It wasn't about earning money for James. It was about building assets that would outlast his playing career. The way he did was by focusing on becoming the best basketball player he could be while having his trusted team look after his business interests. You don't need to reinvent the wheel. Just copy this model and reap the benefits for yourself.

PURCHASES TO AVOID

There are a few types of purchases that every athlete seems to make no matter which sport they're from. Some of these purchases are emotionally driven, while others arise due to a lack of education. Some of them are fueled by debt, while others are bought with cash. This doesn't make their negative impact any lesser. To stay out of debt, you need to tread carefully around these purchases. Not all of them are bad or death sentences. However, they contain pitfalls that you should be aware of before investing.

Jewelry

Blame pop culture and a lack of education for this one. It isn't just athletes but even regular folks who buy jewelry with the aim of "investing" their money. Gaudy chains, rings, bracelets, and watches are like fast food. They taste great in the here and now, but once you're done eating them, you'll feel terrible.

Precious metals are a good investment. Gold, silver, and other metals such as platinum and palladium have proved to be excellent preservers of wealth. Gold has always been a way for the wealthy to preserve their net worth. However, jewelry is not the same as precious metals. This is because each piece of jewelry is customized. Unless you happen to be subject to some very peculiar circumstances, your jewelry will not worth anything.

Diamonds are probably the most overrated form of expense. They have no utility beyond a few industrial applications and behave much like cars do when it comes to their value. Their supply is kept artificially low, and jewelers convince saps to spend three months' income on engagement rings. They shine a lot, which doesn't hurt their appeal. However, your diamonds are worth nothing on the second-hand market. Unlike other forms of jewelry, they can't be melted and turned into something else. Silver and gold jewelry hold their value to a large extent because of this. However, you might as well toss a diamond into a garbage can once you buy it.

This is not to say they're completely worthless. However, they're not as valuable as wealth preservers, as most people believe. A diamond engagement ring is undoubtedly one of the worst ways of using your money.

Cars and Mansions

While most people are smart enough to use cash to buy jewelry, they draw loans to pay for cars and mansions. The reasons for cars being a terrible investment has already been outlined. As for mansions, you've learned how you can create liability by drawing a mortgage. Make sure you fully understand the numbers behind a real estate investment before you sink money into it. Real estate investing involves the use of leverage. This boosts your gains significantly, but it can also sink you if mismanaged.

There are many creative ways of structuring leverage to boost your investment return. However, all of these are risky if you don't understand how they work. For example, you can draw what is called interest-only mortgages that have extremely low monthly payments. The idea is that you finance the property with this mortgage for four years, earn rental income that far outstrips the mortgage payment, and sells the property for a higher value in four years. Why four years? Because the principal kicks in after this period and monthly payments balloon. If mismanaged, this balloon can bankrupt you.

Business Franchises

These can be excellent investments. However, not every business franchise is worth buying. A lot goes into making a successful franchise, and often, even successful businesses in one part of the country struggle to replicate their success elsewhere. For example, just because Papa Johns does well in Denver, this doesn't mean it'll be a hit in New York.

Many athletes invest in businesses they frequent, and this can be a potential mistake as well. Investing should be carried out rationally. Just because you happen to like the pizza at a local pizzeria doesn't mean everyone else will. You need to consider the numbers presented to you and take several other factors into account. I'll cover these in the next chapter.

For now, resist the temptation of investing in a friend's business just because they're close to you. Do not invest in coffee shops, upscale restaurants, nightclubs, and other "cool" businesses. What do I mean by this? If you're buying a business because you think it would be cool to own it, it's probably going to be a bad investment. No one brags about owning a few Subway franchises or a few Krispy Kreme locations. These are boring businesses, but they're precisely the ones that make you money.

Fancy Products

Athletes attract all kinds of people, and there's always someone who has an idea for the next path-breaking invention. These inventions usually break bank accounts, not paths. It's exceptionally hard for someone to launch a new product on the market. Even Steve Jobs got it wrong with some of his investments. The man who invented the iPhone and other jaw-dropping devices was also an investor in the Segway, which was named one of the worst inventions ever (Fletcher, 2010).

Stay away from inventions and new product launches unless you happen to know the market intimately. Even then, it can be tough to get it right. If you want to take a risk, place a small percentage of your investment funds into such an invention. I'm talking less than one percent of your total investment capital. That way, if it does come off, you'll make a massive profit. If it doesn't, you haven't lost much.

CHAPTER 4

INVESTMENTS

It's not how much money you make, but how much money you keep, how hard it works for you, and how many generations you keep it for.

—ROBERT KIYOSAKI

INVESTING your money can be intimidating. There are many options out there, and there are many examples of investments failing. For every instance of someone like Shaq owning 155 Five Guys restaurants, there's Raghib Ismail losing everything on an investment in a Rock n' Roll Cafe.

In this chapter, you're going to learn about the various investment choices you have and how you can make sense of them. There is a common thread that connects every investment evaluation. This is to do with how you evaluate risk. Risk is ever-present, and it's easy to forget how damaging it can be. What is a risk when it comes to investment?

Risk is the probability of you losing all of your money. That's what it comes down to. You can reduce the probability of losing money by educating yourself. This allows you to understand the opportunity fully and evaluate your expected rate of return. Do not get caught up with the potential rewards and neglect risk. For example, let's say you want to open a gamer's cafe. You could look at the rise of esports and gaming in popular culture and decide that there's money to be made there.

Despite the huge potential, you still need to look at the negatives that bring risk to the table. What if your cafe is in a bad location? What if gamers decide to play online and not in physical cafes? What if you can't maintain your locations well enough to entice gamers to keep coming back? Many things contribute to an investment opportunity's risk.

Chief among these is your ability to make the investment work. Many investments are bad choices not because their business models are bad, but because their owners are incapable of executing them. When it comes to your investments, leave the "tough it out" mentality behind you, or on the field. Investment success comes from sticking to what you know and can realistically execute.

You could own a chain of restaurants, but do you have the time to manage the business? Do you have the time to run the books and figure out how each restaurant is doing and whether some are increasingly making losses? If you don't have the time to do this, do you know someone who can run these numbers for you? What will their services cost, and how much do you trust them?

Many athletes don't ask themselves these questions and end up squandering their cash. It would be best if you looked at risk in other dimensions as well. Have you ever noticed that most athletes only seem to place their money in private businesses such as restaurants, cafes, and bakeries? They never seem to brag about their stock market investments. This is because the stock market is completely misunderstood, and it scares away most people.

This is a tragedy because the stock market can make you a lot more money than a private business can. Even better, it can increase your cash flow. A private business only increases your net worth unless it happens to be an already established business. For example, Andre Igoudala has invested a ton of money into private technology companies worth over a billion. These are good investments.

However, they don't add to his cash flow. If he wants to sell his shares, he's not going to get anywhere near what those companies are said to be worth. This is because he'll have to sell it to other company insiders who will squeeze him on the price. It's impossible to know what his financial situation is like. However, if he's taken care of his cash flow needs, these net worth boosting investments are good decisions. If not, he's going to land himself in trouble.

The primary aim of your investments should be to create passive income for yourself. Passive income benefits have been outlined in the first chapter. If you're still not sure of why this is great, please read the first chapter again. Your goal should be to have the majority of your living expenses paid by your passive income. Once you reach this point, you'll be truly free since you won't have to rely on your regular paycheck anymore.

With the goal of passive income generation in mind, let's look at some of the best ways to generate it, with the best options listed first. Despite some of these options being better than others, don't feel as if you "have" to be invested in all of these options. Ultimately, the risk is lowest when you understand the investment. If you don't understand a particular investment method, feel free to stay away from it, and educate yourself as to how it works before opting for it.

REAL ESTATE

Real estate is a great option for many athletes because you won't have many problems qualifying for financing. Financing approval is what trips up regular folks and prevents them from accessing great real estate opportunities. There are a few things to keep in mind when it comes to real estate. Think of these as the basics.

Types of Properties

Broadly speaking, you will find residential and commercial properties. Residential properties are where people live, and commercial properties are where they shop and where companies conduct business. When it comes to investing, it's safest to start in residential properties. This is because there's always a demand for housing, and it's easier to evaluate your tenants. Banks love residential properties for the same reasons, and you won't have issues getting a mortgage.

Should you use a mortgage or buy in cash? This is a good question to consider. If you're in the prime of your career, then it's best to use a mortgage since you can boost your returns massively. While you're in your prime, you have cash coming in, and you should use as much of this cash to invest and grow your wealth. Buying properties with cash eliminates debt risk, but your wealth will grow at a slower pace.

For example, let's say you have your eye on a $100,000 property. If you finance this purchase, you can control the property with $20,000 upfront. If you had to invest $100,000, are you better off investing it across five financed properties adding up to a total of $500,000 or just one property worth $100,000? If you're in your prime and expect to earn money for the next five years or so, the former is a better choice. If you're nearing the end of your career, you want to minimize risk and avoid debt as much as possible. The latter will be a better option for you.

It comes down to how safe your cash flow is. If you feel it's unsafe, then buy with cash. Coming back to residential properties, you can buy single-family or multi-family properties. These indicate how many families live on the property. A single-family home is your typical property in suburbia. In contrast, multifamily properties are multiple units housed within a single structure. Note that apartment blocks are considered commercial properties.

A single-family home can be partitioned and rented out to multiple people. For example, most off-campus housing on college campuses is this kind of property. These properties make for great investments since there will always be a demand for housing from college kids, and you can boost your investment return by renting individual bedrooms instead of the entire home.

Financing

There are a few important terms you need to learn with regards to real estate financing. The first is a down payment. This is the money you pay upfront to the lender to buy the property. The down payment is your equity (remember this from the first chapter?) in the property. Usually, banks will require you to put 20% of the property's value down. They'll loan you 80% of the property's value.

The next term to learn is closing costs. Closing costs are fees you will pay to the various professionals that assist you in completing your purchase. There's a lot that goes on in the background, and these people need to be paid. These costs usually amount to three percent of the property's value. If you buy a property in cash, you'll still need to pay closing costs.

The financing approval process takes anywhere from a month to three months. It gets delayed because banks ask for a ton of documents, and it takes time to procure them if you haven't prepared ahead of time. The best thing to do is speak to a real estate agent who can give you a high-level overview of what will be necessary. Prepare these documents ahead of time and apply for pre-approval. Pre-approval is a bare-bones version of the final approval process, and it speeds up your application when the time will come.

Besides traditional banks, you can apply for Federal Housing Authority (FHA) loans through approved lenders. FHA loans require lower down payments, to the tune of three percent or 10 percent depending on your credit score. However, you will need to live in the property if you wish to use these loans. Carefully consider whether you can monetize such property before opting for it. It's also a good idea to pay more down and build equity when buying a property.

This reduces your monthly mortgage payment and makes it easier for your rental payments to cover all costs. You'll create a better asset. Paying more down also gives you the option of reducing your payment term. Instead of opting for the traditional 30 years, you can aim to pay your property off in 20 years or 15 years if you can manage it. Don't go for the biggest or shiniest home. I'll talk about evaluating properties shortly.

You'll have additional expenses to take care of, such as property insurance (flood, fire, and liability) and property taxes. Taxes are a small percentage of the overall value of the property. However, many people are unaware of how critical they are. They're usually just 1.1% of the home's value, but if you neglect to pay them, you can lose your property. Imagine losing a $200,000 property because you forgot to pay a $2,200 bill at the end of the year! Never forget your taxes. If you don't pay them, the county will auction called a tax lien on your property. A lien is a document that indicates someone has a claim on your property due to unpaid debt. Unpaid taxes are owed to the government, and they come ahead of the mortgage on the property.

This means the government technically has the first claim on your property in case of a payment default (tax payment default). The bank has the next claim (if you have an unpaid balance on your mortgage), and only then do you have a claim to your property. The next time you hear someone talk about how they "own" a million-dollar property, ask them if they have a mortgage and if they've paid their taxes on it.

As long as you have a mortgage on a property, you don't own it. The bank owns it. You have their permission to use it and monetize it. Never forget this. Many real estate investors walk around thinking their property's value can be added to their net worth. This is false. Their equity in the property can be added to their net worth, not the entire value if they have an outstanding mortgage.

You should try to understand this since many investors borrow large sums of cash (draw many mortgages with banks) and think that they're home free since the rental income covers the mortgage payment. This is the case when times are good. What happens when times get rough, and their tenants start losing their jobs? Rental payments dry up, and all of a sudden, their mortgage payments are too much. Bankruptcy and foreclosure are the only way out. It isn't just athletes who fall prey to this; smart real estate investors do so as well. Donald Trump's many bankruptcies resulted from his borrowing too much money and not being able to make payments when the rental income dried up.

So how can you protect yourself? This is where property evaluation plays an important role.

Evaluating Your Investment

The first step to evaluating a property is to ask whether it passes the one percent rule. This rule states that the monthly rental income must be at least one percent of the property's value. For example, if the property is worth $200,000, the monthly rental you can earn must be at least $2,000. Anything below this is not worth it.

Next, you need to estimate costs. Maintenance, utilities, taxes, and vacancies are all costs. Vacancies are an insidious cost since no one considers that their property could lie vacant for extended periods. How can you take all of these costs into account? Simple! Assume that your costs are going to be half of your rental income. If you earn $2,000 in rent, you're going to pay $1,000 per month in costs.

You won't pay this amount every month, but over time, this is what it will average out to. To ensure that this is a reasonable estimate, you need to evaluate the property's qualitative aspects. Location, proximity to urban centers, schools, crime, and neighborhood classification are important factors to consider. It's best to work with a smart agent who can bring you properties that satisfy these criteria. You can even invest in properties that already have tenants in them. These are called turnkey rental properties and provide you with cash flow from the first day.

Educate yourself with regards to evaluating a property. The best resource for this is The Book on Rental Property Investing by Brandon Turner. Turner runs a real estate investment website called BiggerPockets that covers the world of real estate. His book dives into many different forms of rental investing that won't apply to you. Please focus on the chapters where he talks about evaluating properties and the problems to watch out for. Please do not invest in properties until you've read his book. I would detail how to evaluate property locations as well, but it would take me the rest of this book to do so. There are other pressing issues we need to discuss!

STOCK MARKETS

Stock market investing is the second major wealth generator for you. Like real estate investing, it is intimidating and seemingly controlled by big Wall Street banks. This is laughably untrue. The big banks have no more of an idea of what the market will do than you do. The billionaire investor Warren Buffett has regularly said that he has no clue what the market will do tomorrow or over the next decade.

So how can you make money? Making money in the stock market is deceptively simple. All it takes is for you to follow a few simple principles. While they're easy to understand, following them is hard because of how the financial media covers the markets. They focus on the short term and make it seem as if the markets are either rocketing up or spiraling down all the time. They make ludicrous statements such as "Jeff Bezos lost one billion dollars yesterday. Here's how you can "protect yourself" and so on. I've already detailed why this state is false in the first chapter.

Here are some simple principles for you to remember when investing in the stock market:

1. The stock market is simple. Financial institutions make it complex. Ignore them.
2. Minimize your costs of investment. Costs include taxes, inflation (I'll explain this shortly), and commissions.
3. Set and forget your investments. The only exception is if you have a good knowledge of accounting principles and desire to learn all about them to make better investments. Even then, invest passively.
4. Invest in opportunities where you'll keep your money for at least a decade. Anything under a decade is meaningless to you.
5. Invest in instruments you understand. If you cannot understand it, do not invest, no matter how much money you can potentially make or how stupid someone thinks you are.
6. Do not fool yourself. Be honest about your

abilities. Avoid stupidity instead of trying to be clever.

These principles are the same as those that Buffett and a host of other famous investors such as Bill Ackman and Ray Dalio have espoused. They're active investors, but you'll see that it applies to pretty much any form of investing if you read these principles again. Point 4 might not always apply to an active investor. However, you aim to set and forget your investments. You don't want to lose sleep or get distracted by them.

Here is the easiest strategy to follow.

Index Investing

An index is a collection of stocks that have something in common with them. Indexes are created by large financial corporations such as Standard and Poors and Moodys. If you've read anything about the stock market, you will have come across the S&P 500. This is an index that approximates overall market performance. It consists of the 500 biggest companies in America and tracks their performance. Each stock's performance to the index is added, giving the index a value that can be tracked.

Here's a simple example. Let's say you have a three stock index. Each of these stocks is priced at $10, $20, and $50. Add these up, and you have an index value of $80. Let's say tomorrow; these stocks sell for $5, $30, and $40. The index value is $75. The S&P 500's calculation is complex, but this is the essence of it. You do not have to figure out how the index is calculated. What's important is for you to recognize the power of an index.

The S&P 500 used to look very different back in 1926 when it was first established. Back then, railroads and heavy manufacturing companies dominated it. In the 1950s, the railroads steadily vanished as manufacturing and chemical companies dominated it. By the 1970s, the manufacturing companies began faltering, and banks took their place. By the 1990s, manufacturing companies vanished, and financial firms dominated the index and fledgling technology companies. Today, the index is dominated by technology companies such as Apple, Google, and Amazon.

What's the lesson here? Despite the individual sectors facing ups and downs over the past century, the S&P 500 has always managed to capture the best-performing companies. This is because its criteria are simple. The 500 biggest companies get in, irrespective of which industry they're active in. This has resulted in the index gaining an average of 10% every year since its inception. It hasn't risen by this amount like clockwork, but this is the average performance.

The lesson here is that instead of predicting what the fortunes of individual companies might be, it's better to bet on the broader stock market index. America's economic position is strong enough that its companies will remain at the forefront of the industrial revolution for the foreseeable future. Despite China's rise and occasional news about how pretenders like India and Brazil are rising, America's dominance remains unquestioned.

This means all you need to do is invest in the index, and your money will grow over time. The problem is that you cannot buy an index. It isn't a tradable instrument. However, you can buy funds that track indexes.

Index Funds and Exchange Traded Funds

An index fund is an instrument that is run by a fund manager. The manager buys all the stocks present in an index and aims to track the index's performance. For example, you can buy an index fund that tracks the S&P 500. By doing this, you'll closely replicate the index's performance in your portfolio. All you'll need to do is make one purchase to buy units of the index fund.

The S&P 500 isn't the only index you can track. Other indexes include those that track foreign stock markets, real estate markets, bond markets, and dividend-paying stocks. Investing in dividend-paying stocks' indexes makes the most sense, from the standpoint of investment simplicity.

A dividend is a cash distribution that a company makes to its shareholders. They usually pay a sum of cash that will amount to a maximum of five to six percent of the stock's price. This is called the yield. For example, if a company's stock is selling for $100 and pays a $4 dividend, it's yielding four percent (4/100). Higher yields are attainable, to the tune of 15% and above. The problem is that declining stock prices usually cause higher yields.

From the previous example, if the company paid $4 the previous year and if its stock price declines to $50, its current yield will be (4/50) eight percent. This looks great on paper, but a declining stock price produces it.

This is not good news for investors. It indicates there's something wrong with the company and that their money might not be safe. It's far better to focus on investing in index funds that track dividend-paying stock indexes.

Two major indexes track dividends you should pay attention to. The first is the Dividend Aristocrats index. This index screens stocks that have paid a dividend for at least 25 years. Not only should these companies have paid a dividend for this time, but they also need to have increased their payouts consistently. These companies are extremely safe and will probably be around forever. Even if they don't, the index will screen in the new top-performing companies. Businesses such as Coca Cola, Johnson & Johnson, and P&G are a part of this index.

The second index is the Dividend Achievers index. This index's criteria are the same, except the period of dividend payment and increases are ten years, not 25. This index captures more growth-oriented companies since the period is low. You can buy index funds that track this index as well.

By buying an index fund, you'll make just one purchase that will give you exposure to an entire world of dividend-paying stocks. The reason dividends are powerful is because you get paid cash for your investment. A typical dividend index fund yields two percent. This means you're going to earn at least two percent on your investment every year. This is your cash flow. Your net worth will be boosted by how much ever the price increases every year.

Prices are not guaranteed to increase every year, and

this is why it's important to remain invested for a long period. You cannot hope to earn the average 10% gain in the index over a period of five years or so. Aim to remain invested for over 15 years and do not withdraw this money under any circumstances.

Keep contributing to this account regularly, and your money will grow over time. How much can you grow it to over 20 years? Let's use the calculator at http://www.moneychimp.com/calculator/compound_interest_calculator.htm to figure this out. Let's assume you invest $12,000 in the first year. This is equal to $1,000 per month, which is attainable if you're fiscally prudent, as described previously.

You will contribute this amount every year for 20 years, and your investment will grow at an average of 10% during this time, every year. How much will you be left with? Plugging these numbers into the calculator, we see that our ending principal will be $768,029. What happens if you remain invested for 25 years? you'll have $1,310,181.

If you live on 40% of your income and save 60% of it, you can contribute a lot more than $1,000 per month. Let's say you earn $5,000 per month after taxes and live on $3,000 per month. This results in you saving 40% of your income, which is $2,000. If you contribute this amount to your investment account, how much will you have at the end of 25 years? The answer is $2,620,362.

Your objective should be to generate enough passive income from your prime earning days so that most of your investment contribution will come from this. Let's say you buy a property in cash and invest the rental proceeds in the stock market. You continue to live off your active income. Once your playing days are over, you can work a regular job that pays most of your bills, and your passive income covers the gap. Your investment contributions can continue, even if they're reduced.

By the age of 60 or 65, you'll have more than a million dollars in your investment account. I'll discuss how to live off this income in the next chapter, where I'll discuss retirement options. Index fund investing will get you to this level easily. Index funds aren't the only investment option you have.

Exchange-traded funds or ETFs are also managed funds. The difference is that ETF prices move during the day, unlike index fund prices, and they don't have investment minimums. The typical index fund has investment minimums of $3,000. This is not the case with ETFs. You can buy ETFs that employ an index tracking strategy. You can get adventurous with ETFs but avoid the complex ones.

Coming back to dividend investing, you have the option of reinvesting your dividends into your investments. This is called a Dividend reinvestment Program or DRIP. DRIPs can boost your investment gains massively. In the previous scenario, we assumed that your investment would grow at 10% per year. This gain is achieved through increases in the price of the index fund or the ETF. This is called a capital gain. Dividends are cash-flow gains. They put two percent (in the case of most ETFs and index funds) in your pocket every year.

You can reinvest this two percent and grow the amount of principal you're investing every year for free.

ETFs and index funds charge fees for the services they provide. Do not pay more than 0.05% of your principal as fees every year. Some of the most reputable ETF issues, such as Vanguard and iShares, charge around 0.02% of your principal as fees. This is an extremely reasonable fee to pay.

Investment Accounts

When investing in the stock market, you have two options. You can invest through a retirement account or a normal account. Most professional sports leagues in America offer what is called a 401(k) retirement account. Under the terms of this account, you can direct a portion of your pre-tax income to an investment of your choice. Best of all, your employer (the league) will match this contribution up to a certain percentage.

For example, let's say you're earning $100,000 per year before taxes. This is roughly $8,333 per month. You can divert $2,000 per month to an investment account containing your ETF or index fund holdings. Your employer will usually match 40% of this amount and will deposit the money into your account. This means you'll receive $800 per month for free.

I'll cover retirement accounts in more depth in the next chapter. For now, understand that you won't pay taxes on your gains or dividends until you withdraw the money at the age of 60. It would help if you tried to collect as much free money from your employer as you can through matching contributions. Make it your aim to contribute so much to your retirement account that your employer will feel the need to pull you aside and tell you to take it easy! They're legally obliged to match a percentage of your contributions, so it's not as if they can stop you from doing it.

Retirement accounts have contribution limits, so you'll need to open a regular investment account with a broker. Brokers offer many different accounts, namely, cash accounts, margin accounts, options trading accounts, and commodity investment accounts. Opt for a cash account. You don't need any of the other stuff to invest successfully.

You'll have to pay taxes on your gains, and I'll cover this topic two chapters from now. Taxation isn't too complicated, so don't worry about this too much. Your broker will provide you with all the forms you need. Many brokers these days offer zero commission trades, so you don't have to worry about paying high commissions. If you happen to trade regularly (multiple times every day), then you'll pay commissions. However, as you've learned already, all you need to do is invest a lump sum every month and leave it at that.

Opening a brokerage account is straightforward. You can choose an app such as Robinhood or a full-service brokerage such as Charles Schwab. Discount brokers such as Firstrade also offer you all the necessary services. When picking a broker, make sure they're registered with the Financial Services Authority (FINRA).

That's all there is to stock market investing. As you can see, it's extremely simple and automatic. People love to overcomplicate things, and this is why they lose money. Don't worry about what the market is doing in the short term. Let the financial news scream about how bad things are. Your objective is to remain invested over a period of 20 years or more. Start as quickly as you can and remain invested for a long as possible.

I must state that it's important for you to get rid of debt and establish your financial freedom fund before investing in the market. The objective of this investment is not to touch the money until you're retired. Without these prerequisites, you'll be likely to withdraw your money, and this will hurt its growth. Avoid this as much as possible. This is why you should invest money that you will not miss. This way, there's very little chance of you having to withdraw this money.

Please do not invest in the stock market with the intention of having it pay for your property's down payment or any other expense. The stock market isn't a lottery ticket, so don't treat it this way. Follow the sound investment principles that I've outlined in this chapter, and you'll be just fine.

Gold, Silver and so on

Precious metals can be good investments but don't invest the majority of your portfolio into them. It's best to invest five percent of your portfolio into gold ETFs and leave it at that. The same applies to cryptocurrencies as well. Remember that your investment in these alternative assets shouldn't exceed more than 10% of your overall portfolio, with five percent being optimal.

This is because these assets fluctuate a lot. They're

also not backed by anything real like stocks are. A stock represents a business that has office space, employees, earnings, customers, and inventory. Cryptocurrency has nothing backing it other than the feelings of many people. As long as the feeling persists, their values remain high. Once the bubble pops, it's all worthless. The same applies to gold as well. You can debate till kingdom come about how long the feeling that drives these assets' values will last. However, the point is that feelings are not tangible things. You can't invest based on feelings, so avoid or minimize this.

As for other commodities such as oil or agricultural products, stay well away from them. These are intensely speculative assets, and they fluctuate a lot. You're best served to avoid stupidity, instead of trying to be too smart. Recall this is one of the primary rules of successful investing. Stay within the bounds of what you know, and you'll be successful. Let other people experiment with their money. Your objective is to be as boring as possible. This is what will help you sleep well at night.

PRIVATE BUSINESSES

Private business investments should be last on your order of priorities. This is because they're extremely hard to extricate yourself from in case things go wrong. Let's say your real estate investment goes wrong, and you want to get out of it. You can place your property on the market and receive offers for it within a reasonable period. If a stock market investment goes bad or if you want to withdraw your money, all you need to do is click a button. You'll get your money back, even if it isn't the amount you invested.

With private businesses, you don't have such options. Your business is not traded on the stock exchange, and it's hard to convince regular people to buy your shares in the business. You'll most probably have to sell them to other business people who will squeeze you on the price. There's also the fact that a business is not an easy thing to execute. The majority of businesses fail because of how hard it is.

No matter how great a business idea sounds, the odds are stacked against it. A common trap most people, including athletes, fall into is to invest in businesses that sound cool or have an emotional pull. Examples of these businesses are cafes, fancy restaurants, nightclubs, and other places of entertainment. People think these ventures are profitable because they like the idea of calling themselves owners of successful establishments such as these.

However, all of these businesses are terrible investments because their economics are bad. Why would anyone choose a neighborhood cafe over a Starbucks? Most fancy restaurants close within a year of opening in the United States (*Restaurant Profitability and Failure Rates: What You Need to Know | FSR Magazine,* 2019). As for nightclubs, their appeal is extremely short-lived. Most club owners shut shop and rebrand their venues within a few months.

Successful athletes have many people looking to

become freeloaders. These people almost always have these kinds of harebrained business ideas. Establish investments in either of the two categories above (real estate and the stock market) before considering an investment in a private venture.

Technology and apps have become hot thanks to the digital economy. Do not invest in any company you cannot understand. I'll detail the investment criteria you must follow shortly. These apply to all kinds of businesses. If you wish to invest in a business, you need to understand that private businesses are rarely passive. You will need to be involved in them regularly, and they can turn into a full-time job. If this is your aim, then feel free to invest in them. However, please don't assume that they're your only option.

Franchises are the best investment you can make. Not only will you gain the brand power of a successful business, but you'll also receive advice from the business with regards to business best practices. This doesn't mean franchise investments aren't risk-free. It's just that your risk is lower with this option than choosing to start a business of your own. It's not a coincidence that some of the most successful athlete investments have been in successful franchises.

I've already highlighted the example of Shaquille O'Neal and his Five Guys and Krispy Kreme investments. He's also on the board of Papa John's pizza and is a former franchisee. LeBron James successfully invested in Blaze Pizza and helped it become a national chain. This is an example of an investment that is hard to replicate. James invested in a small, local pizza chain that happened to go national. Don't seek to replicate this level of success. I'm not saying this to be pessimistic. It's just that there are easier ways to grow your wealth. Peyton Manning is another example of an athlete who invested in several Papa John's franchises in Denver. He promptly sold them right before the brand was dropped by the NFL and cashed in right at the top.

Franchise business models work pretty much the same way, no matter what the brand is. The franchise (you) needs to pay a certain amount of money to the brand to acquire the rights to use their name at that location. You'll have to pay the rent as well as all expenses related to interior design and inventory (in the case of a fast-food joint, this will be food). From the revenue you earn every month, you'll need to pay royalty fees to the franchise and follow their business operations guidelines.

The advantage is that you can instantly copy and past successful business practices without reinventing the wheel. The brand name alone guarantees some recognition and business. Usually, brands will support their franchisees if the business is slow. It won't be monetary support, but they will boost advertising in your area to drive traffic, along with offering you special promotions. You'll be responsible for staff hiring and salaries. The bottom line profit for most franchisees is between seven to 10% of revenues.

If you own a Krispy Kreme location that sells $1,000 worth of goods every day, this translates to $365,000 worth of sales every year. You can expect to earn $36,500 every year in profits from this location. These numbers are indicative and are for illustration purposes only. You'll need to run the numbers yourself to figure out how much you can earn.

The best way to run these locations is to invest in hiring a business manager. This person will run the day to day operations of your locations and will manage their finances. You'll need to check in with them every week to make sure everything is running smoothly. It's best to hire people from within your network or to hire those who have prior experience. Check with your accountant to find such people. Your accountant will also help you set up a business entity that will safeguard your business interests and ensure your assets are not tied to your business's fortunes. Remember that such investments come after you've got rid of your debt, saved up enough for a freedom fund, and established a real estate stream of income or an investment in the stock market.

Here are a few tips that will help you figure out the investment value of any business.

Do You Understand it?

When someone explains the business to you, do you understand it? Many people invest in businesses they don't understand due to the fear of missing out. They think if they miss this opportunity, they'll never find another investment of the kind. This is incorrect. There are abundant opportunities to grow your money, so don't ever think that you "have" to invest in something.

When examining the business, ask yourself if you can

run it yourself. The best business can be run easily. Remember that with investments, your objective is to avoid risk at all costs. If the worst comes to happen and if your manager turns out to be a moron, can you step in and reasonably run the business? If so, invest in it.

Simple Products

What are the products or services that the business offers? Do they have universal appeal? Food is a no-brainer investment. Certain technology apps can also be of this nature; however, make sure you understand them well. Complicated products that require explanation are never good investments. If you can't understand why you'd want to own one, how can you expect someone else to understand them?

Make it a point to examine the investments of other successful people. This is what Shaq did. He's mentioned in the past that he heard Jeff Bezos say that the best investments are the ones that change people's lives and affect them to a great degree. Educate yourself and consume content around investment principles. You'll find yourself learning a lot by emulating the examples of other successful people.

Margins

Margin refers to the amount of money you can earn from the business. Gross margin refers to the difference between a product's cost price and its selling price. A product that costs $10 to make and $20 to sell has a 50% margin. A product that costs $10 to make and $50 to sell has an 80% margin. Net margin refers to whatever is left over after all expenses, including salaries, rental expenses, utilities, and taxes are accounted for. In the case of the $50 product, if you pay $10 in rent, $5 in utilities, $10 as salaries, and $5 as taxes, your total costs are:

Total costs = Product purchase cost + rent utilities + salaries + taxes = 10+10+5+10+5 = $40

Net margin = (Revenues up on sale - total costs)/Revenues = (50-40)/50 = 20%

Gross margins for services are harder to compute. In these cases, examining the net margin is better. Often, when being pitched business ideas, you'll be shown the gross margin figures. Someone might come up to you and say you can buy shoes for $10 in China and sell them for $60 in the United States. You'll earn $50 per shoe, which is 500% of your investment ($50 is your profit, which is 500% of $10). This makes it sound like a wonderful investment. However, this calculation is the wrong way to look at the business. First, ask yourself what the gross margin is. In this case, it's 83%, which is very healthy.

Next, ask yourself what the costs involved in selling the shoe are. You'll need retail space, employees, marketing, electronic systems to track sales, warehouses to store inventory, supply chain systems to ensure inventory is well stocked, and lastly, you'll need to pay taxes. All of these will eat into that gross margin and give you a much lower net margin.

Compare

This step will save you from a world of pain. The net margin of a business is what ultimately goes into your pocket as a business owner. This is what your money is earning. If a business offers you a net margin of just five percent, it makes zero sense for you to invest in it. Why? Because you have your real estate and stock market investments. These are paying you a higher rate of return.

It makes no sense to invest in something that grows your money at a rate below what you can reasonably expect to earn through your other investment methods. You don't need a million different investments to be successful. As Warren Buffett routinely says, you need just two or three very good investments to become wealthy. Focus on quality, not quantity.

SAVINGS ACCOUNTS

You might be wondering why I haven't spoken of savings accounts as being legitimate investment options? Well, this has to do with the rate of return they offer. The average savings account offers a paltry sub-one percent return in America right now. This is better than nothing, of course, but it doesn't grow your wealth.

The reason is inflation. Inflation is a hidden cost that all of your investments need to overcome. Currently, the United States experiences inflation of 1.3% per year (*Current US Inflation Rates: 2009-2019*, 2019). This means everything becomes 1.3% more expensive every year. This sounds like a bad thing, but it's quite healthy. An economy that is growing in prosperity will experience healthy inflation levels.

The opposite of inflation is deflation, which indicates that the economy is shrinking and businesses are shutting down on a large scale. An exaggerated version of inflation if hyperinflation, where prices rise uncontrollably. This happens because of economic mismanagement. In the United States, inflation is expected to rise to at least two percent over the next decade. It might even hit four percent.

This means your investments need to grow at this rate at the very least to have an impact. If your savings account pays you less than one percent and if inflation is around 1.3%, you're losing money. This is why you should keep just your freedom cash in your savings account. Put the rest in places where it will grow.

CHAPTER 5

RETIREMENT PLANNING

The question isn't at what age I want to retire, it's at what income.

—GEORGE FOREMAN

WHEN YOU'RE YOUNG, you feel invincible, and retirement seems like a world away. I'm not talking about retiring from the sport you play. I'm talking about actual retirement when your body won't be in the best of shape anymore, and your ability to carry out physical tasks will be compromised. This is the age when injuries will catch up to you, and you'll need additional assistance to live well.

What makes retirement tricky for athletes is that their playing days finish in their early thirties. However, real retirement kicks in only once they turn 60. That's a gap of close to 30 years that's difficult to bridge with just your income from your playing days. If you were lucky enough to earn multimillion-dollar deals in your prime, then you'll have enough to last you a lifetime. Most athletes don't earn anywhere near this kind of money, though.

THE FIRST RETIREMENT

Successful retirement planning begins before your playing days are over. The average person can afford to start retirement planning in their forties, but you don't have this luxury. You don't have to think about what life will be like when you're 60, but you need to develop plans for a second career. It's very unlikely that you'll be able to stretch your income from your playing days till retirement. Besides, it's not as if your life is going to end at 60. You can expect to live till you're 80, at the very least.

A second career can involve several things. You could consider coaching or instruction in your sport. Broadcasting is another option that many former athletes use. If you have writing skills, you could consider writing a column for a major magazine and bring insight into your sport. This is what Ross Tucker, a former NFL lineman, did. A journeyman player in the league, injury finally put an end to his career. This led him to chronicle the experience in the noted journalist Peter King's sports column in sports Illustrated. The overwhelming response convinced

Tucker to go full time with his writing, and he now hosts his podcast.

If you think you have the chops to be a broadcaster, it's best to start preparing right now. You can easily start your podcast, and bringing guests onto your show won't be an issue thanks to your active connections. Add this to social media exposure on Instagram and Twitter, and you've got yourself a great second career. Who knows, you might even become the next John Madden. Many people forget that Madden was a Super Bowl-winning coach with the Raiders. Before that, he was a pro football player before an injury ended his career.

Another great example of the second and third acts is Steve Spurrier. He's largely known for his time as the University of Florida's football program's head coach. Few remember that he won the Heisman Trophy as a collegiate athlete. He's now a broadcaster on Sirius XM for SEC football games. These are exceptional examples, of course.

Some athletes start successful second careers as business owners. Former NFL linebacker Brian Orakpo and his former teammate, safety Michael Griffin, are currently the owners of a cupcake shop, which is the last place you'd expect a couple of burly defensive football players to end up. My point with all of these stories is to illustrate that there are always options. It's up to you to sit down and pick the one that appeals to you the most.

There isn't a single path you can take, and this is a good thing. It means you have options. Many athletes decide to return to their alma mater and join the coaching staff. Take the case of Anthony Schlegel, a former linebacker at Ohio State University and the NFL. Following a lackluster professional career, Schlegel joined Ohio State's coaching staff and was struck with an idea for a training machine that players could use.

He quit the staff, got himself an MBA, and patented The Striking Machine. Schlegel is now a successful inventor and runs The Difference USA which markets strength-related products to football programs. All of these stories illustrate the many paths life can take you on once you've left the game. There's no reason for you to be afraid of life after your first career.

If nothing particularly creative strikes you, you can always go back to your alma mater and study for a degree. Universities are very welcoming of former athletes and, in many cases, provide free education or heavily discounted ones. Universities are not the only sources of education. If you happen to be interested in technology and programming, you can study online and join coding boot camps.

Make a list of the things you're passionate about and that you can envision yourself doing 10 or 20 years down the line. Make it a goal to have your new source of active income provide you with at least enough money to cover all of your living expenses. Remember, you'll have set up sources of passive income earlier, so it's not as if you won't have any money coming in.

Begin exploring your options before you retire from your sport. Talk to players who've been through this experience and study examples of former athletes successfully making the transition. If your league has support resources that can help you transition to off-field life, use them. Remember that you don't have to do this all by yourself. Lean of those close to you and seek their help. If your partner or spouse can work at a job, this will bring in additional income.

It's important for the two of you to work as a team and figure out what you want your off-field life to look like. If you're faced with the prospect of living in conditions that are below what you've grown accustomed to, then start planning for it right now. Are you okay with this transition, or do you want to maintain the same standard of living? Not everyone is as lucky as Tony Romo is and can earn more as a broadcaster than they did as a player.

Remember that a decrease in living standards doesn't mean you'll be giving up luxuries forever. You'll need those luxuries when you retire due to old age—plan for those years right now by utilizing all of the investment options available to you.

Retirement Accounts

There are two kinds of retirement accounts you can open. The first is an Individual Retirement Account or IRA. There are two types of IRAs, called the traditional IRA and the Roth IRA. The second type of retirement account is a 401(k), which you were briefly introduced to previously. Let's deal with IRAs first.

IRAs are called tax-deferred accounts. The way they work is simple. All of the money you invest in an IRA is non-taxable until you reach 59 ½. You can withdraw your money at this age and will have to pay taxes on your withdrawal at ordinary income tax rates. I'll explain the deal with taxes in the next chapter. Ordinary income tax rates are the same as the taxes you pay on your current earnings.

If you withdraw your money before the age of 59 ½, you will pay a penalty of 10% of your withdrawal amount, and you'll pay taxes on the withdrawal. Once you reach the age of 70, you'll be forced to withdraw money from your IRA. There are minimum amounts of money you'll have to withdraw every year after this age.

The benefits of an IRA lie mostly in their ability to defer taxes. If you buy a stock for $10 and sell it for $20, you don't need to pay taxes on it if you've done this in an IRA account. A regular broker will help you open an IRA without any issues, so it's not as if you'll have to deal with a mountain of paperwork. The biggest benefit of a traditional IRA is that you'll be contributing pre-tax dollars to this account. For example, you could allocate $2,000 of your pre-tax income to your IRA account and invest this into the market. You'll, therefore, not pay income tax on this amount before investing it.

Let's look at the potential gains via an example. Let's say you receive $2,000 as income. You'll have to pay taxes on this. Let's say you pay 10% as taxes. This reduces your income available to $1,800. You invest this money into stocks and let's say, after a year, you earn a gain of 10%. You decide to sell your investment, at which point you'll need to pay taxes. For simplicity's sake, let's say this tax rate is also 10%. You're now left with:

Initial investment = $1,800
Gain = 10% of $1,800 = $180
New balance before taxes = initial investment + gain = $1,980
Tax rate = 10%
Tax amount = 10% of gains = 180*.1 = $18
New balance after taxes = Balance before taxes - tax amount = 1980 - 18 = $1,962

Let's assume you invest this new amount into another opportunity that nets you 10% once again. You'll again pay 10% in taxes. Your new balance is now:

Initial investment = $1,962
Gain = 10% of $1,800 = $196.2
New balance before taxes = initial investment + gain = $2,158.2
Tax rate = 10%
Tax amount = 10% of gains = 180*.1 = $19.62
New balance after taxes = Balance before taxes - tax amount = 2,158.2 - 19.62 = $2,138.58

You're still making money, but as you can see, you received $2,000 before taxes initially, and in two years, you've grown this to $2,138.58. How would this picture change if you had contributed $2,000 into an IRA? Your contribution is non-taxable, so that you would have deposited the full $2,000 into the account.

After the first year, this would have grown to $2,200. There are no taxes to be paid if you sell this investment. You would have invested this entire amount into the second investment and gained 10% on that to leave you with $2,420 at the end of the second year. This is compared to $2,139 in the case of taxable income. That's a difference of 12% over just two years. Let's say this picture remains the same till you reach the age of 69 ½. You'll pay taxes on the withdrawal. Once again, let's assume this is 10%. Your overall gain has been (2,420-2,000) $420. 10% of this is $42. Your final amount after taxes is $2,378.

This is 11% greater than the case where you invested taxable income. Using an IRA has made you 11% more money, and this is just over two years. Over the course of 20 or 25 years, you can expect far greater gains. IRA contributions are currently capped at $6,000 per year, which doesn't sound like much (Retirement Topics - IRA Contribution Limits | Internal Revenue Service, 2019). However, given how they boost your gains, it makes sense to contribute this amount in full.

Roth IRAs work a bit differently than traditional IRAs. For starters, you cannot contribute pre-tax dollars into a Roth. Your post-tax income can be contributed and will not attract any taxes until withdrawal at the age of 59 ½ and above. Roth contribution limits are the same as traditional IRAs. However, they depend on your filing type and income (Retirement Topics - IRA Contribution Limits | Internal Revenue Service, 2019). You should check with your accountant or with the IRS to figure out the latest information since this changes every year.

The advantage of a Roth IRA is that you don't need to pay taxes on your earnings for certain types of withdrawals. If you're withdrawing your money after you're 59 ½ years old, and if you have a permanent disability, or if your beneficiary is withdrawing the money after your death, or if you're withdrawing a sum of $100,000 to build your first home, these withdrawals are tax-free.

Note that only your earnings are tax-free. Your contributions are not taxed, unlike the case with a traditional IRA. For example, let's say you invested $6,000 into an IRA and $6,000 into a Roth IRA. Let's assume both of these investments grew to $6,600, at which point you've decided to withdraw them once you reach the age of 60.

With the traditional IRA, the tax authorities will add the $6,600 to your overall income and ask you to pay taxes according to the relevant tax bracket you fit into. If you earned $55,000 during the year, your taxable income would be (55,000+6,000) $61,000. This is not the case with the Roth IRA. If you earned $55,000 during the year, your taxable income would be this amount plus whatever gains your investment experienced.

Thus, you'll pay taxes on (55,000+600) $55,600. This results in a lower tax bill. The reason for this is your contributions to a Roth IRA have already been taxed before they were deposited. In contrast, the ones to your traditional IRA weren't. Remember how you diverted them before you received any money? Speak to a financial advisor to determine which choice is better for you. A lot depends on your financial situation, so it's best to seek professional help.

Let's leave the world of IRAs behind for now and examine the 401(k). As you've already learned, these retirement accounts provide you the benefit of employer matching. Take full advantage of this since this is free money. Happily, 401(k) contribution limits are much higher than IRAs. The annual limit is $19,500.

401(k)s can also be traditional or Roth, depending on the type of contributions you're making. Given the advantages of employer matching, making pre-tax contributions is the best move forward. Maximize these contributions and employer matching, and you'll earn a ton of money over time. It's not very common these days, but some leagues offer managed 401(k) plans. The idea is that your league contracts an investment firm to manage the assets in the 401(k).

You can opt for these but make sure you have your passive investments setup as described before. If you end up having more than one employer, then you can have two 401(k) plans but your overall contribution per year needs to be under the limit. If you feel confused by these options, consult a financial advisor, and ask them for help.

YOUR SECOND RETIREMENT

At some point in time, you're going to have to figure out what kind of life you want after you turn 60. You can continue to work after that age, but physically, you're going to face limitations. Some of your old injuries will catch up, and you might need physical assistance. Most people usually start planning for this phase of life in their forties, and it will most likely be the same for you as well.

Take some time and make a list of all the things you

want in your life at that age. Where will you live? What will you do during the day, and how will you occupy yourself? If you plan on traveling, then you need to account for these costs as well. Involve your partner and discuss everything with them in detail.

By that age, you'll have paid off your properties and will own them fully. You will have enough income coming in passively to give you steady cash flow. Cash flow is extremely important when you retire because it increases your net worth or paper money doesn't serve you anymore. What is the use of you worth a billion on paper if you don't have the cash to pay your medical bills? Besides, you can only leave your heirs so much money. There's no point continuing to accumulate large gains on paper unless you're truly interested in doing so.

You can shift your portfolio towards income-generating strategies. Dividend investing is one way of doing this. Instead of reinvesting your dividends, you could elect to receive them as cash. You can invest in bond ETFs that will pay you a certain amount of money every year. Perhaps the best retirement solution is an annuity.

Annuities are offered by insurance companies and are a great way to receive a pension in retirement. There are different types of annuities, but all of them work on the same basic premise. They work because you pay the insurance company a certain sum of money and tell them when you wish to start receiving monthly payments and how much you want those payments to be. Depending on these conditions, you'll have to invest a certain amount of cash.

The longer you choose to delay payments, and the older you are, the higher your monthly payments will be. You can choose different kinds of payout structures as well. You can choose to have them pay you till the end of your lifetime, beyond the end of your life to your heirs or spouse until the money you invested runs out, the payout for a minimum number of years (usually 10) and then refund you the remaining amount, or pay you till the end of your life and then refund you the remaining amount.

As you can see, there are several combinations, so it's best to talk to a financial advisor and understand your options. Start preparing in your forties, so that you'll have a steady stream of cash when you're older. Annuities don't provide you with the highest return rates on your money, but they provide you steady cash flow. As you reach the end of your life, growing money isn't much of a concern as receiving cash to live is.

If everything has gone according to plan, you'll have a decent number of assets to look after in your old age. As you take stock of how things are likely to pan out when you're 40, you need to think about drafting a will and planning these assets' disposal. By disposal, I don't mean selling them. Instead, think about how you'd like to deal with them. You can pass them onto your heirs, or you could sell it and invest that money elsewhere.

If you have the cash, you should also consider setting up a trust fund for your children or heirs. The way it works is much like an annuity. You invest a sum of money, and your heirs get paid a fixed amount of cash every month after reaching a certain age. How much you want them to be paid every month depends on you. You could go the Warren Buffett way and leave them with close to nothing, or you could go the Bill Gates way and leave them with just enough not to be poor but not so much that they won't need to work for a living.

Your health will be of major concern as you grow old, so you should take the time to schedule regular doctor's visits and prepare to address any injuries that will worsen. Knees and ankles are usually what goes first, especially if you've played a contact sport. Consider whether you'll need a mobility scooter once you're older and plan on investing in one right now. This could be as simple as checking which insurers provide this facility and how much it will cost.

You might also need to look at your living arrangements and make changes to your home. If need be, you might have to move to a new home to facilitate your new lifestyle. It will be tough to think of everything this much in advance but remember to view everything through the prism of risk. Work to mitigate risk as much as possible, and you're less likely to deal with nasty surprises.

Like with investing, proper retirement planning is a question of educating yourself. Speak to counselors and use the help of organizations to advise you on the best move for your future. Just like with all of your endeavors on the field, prepare as much as possible in advance, and you'll be well set to handle retirement and all of its challenges. The most important thing is for you to get serious about it.

Unlike regular people, you have two retirements to

deal with. It can be hard to say goodbye to the game you've played since you were a kid but don't overstay your welcome and put your body at greater risk than strictly needed. The injuries you sustain today will present their bill when you're older. Speak to older players in your sport to gain perspective on how you can take better care of yourself.

Your first retirement will give you a good perspective on your second. When you retire from your playing days, you'll be tempted to think of yourself as old, but in terms of regular life, you're just entering your prime. The average retirement age of an athlete is around 31 years old. In the real world, a 31-year-old is just getting started on the prime of their lives. Never forget this. You're not old. You've just achieved a lot at a very young age.

You're now all set to achieve even more, which will prepare you to live peacefully and well during your old age. Prepare all the way, and you'll be just fine.

CHAPTER 6

TAXES

Our new Constitution is now established, everything seems to promise it will be durable; but, in this world, nothing is certain except death and taxes.

—BENJAMIN FRANKLIN

CONTRARY TO WHAT you might be expecting, this chapter isn't going to be too long. I understand that taxes can be dry and boring, and they often consume numerous volumes. Well, none of that is going to happen here. As far as taxes go, they're quite simple to deal with as long as you follow the rules and don't get too adventurous.

There are two levels of taxes you'll have to deal with. The first is personal tax, and the second is business tax. Let's look at personal taxes first.

PERSONAL INCOME TAXES

There are two types of personal income tax you will pay. The first is ordinary income tax, and the second is capital gains taxes. Here's where it can get confusing. Capital gains taxes, which you pay on investment gains, are of two types, short-term and long-term. If you held your investment for less than a year before selling it, this is a short term investment. Short term capital gains taxes are equal to ordinary income taxes. Long term capital gains taxes, applicable on investments you help for more than a year before selling, are lower than ordinary income taxes and depend on your regular income.

Ordinary income tax rates are determined based on the tax bracket you fall into and how you're filing your taxes. You can file taxes as an individual, jointly with your spouse, separately with your spouse (it makes no sense in English, but the tax code has its own weird rules) and as a head of a household. The brackets have minimum and maximum incomes and a tax rate that goes along with them. For example, if you file as a single person, all income you earn up to $9,875 will be taxed at 10%.

For the latest income tax brackets, you can visit https://www.nerdwallet.com/article/taxes/federal-income-tax-brackets. This link will provide you with the relevant tables to detail your tax rate according to your filing status. Something to note about these tax brackets is that they're progressive. Let's say you earn $50,000 per year. The first $9,875 is taxed at 10%, the next $40,125 is taxed at 12%, and the remaining amount is taxed at 22%.

The income you earn in the form of cash flow will be taxed at ordinary income tax rates. For example, the rental cash flow that you earn will be taxed as ordinary income. Suppose you draw a salary for yourself from your business or pay yourself a dividend. In that case, it is taxed as ordinary income. There are ways to lower your tax bill using a business; I'll discuss business taxation shortly.

Capital gains occur when you sell an asset for a higher price than what you bought it for. If you buy a stock for $10 and sell it for $20 a year later, you'll pay long-term capital gains taxes on the profit you earned from the sale. Long term capital gains tax rates are significantly lower than ordinary income tax rates. This is why it makes sense to hang onto your investments for at least one year. Not only does this give your investment more time to grow, but it also reduces your tax bill massively. Of course, the ideal timeline is greater than ten years since it takes this long for any asset to appreciate.

Long term capital gains tax rates can be found at this link: https://www.investopedia.com/articles/personal-finance/101515/comparing-longterm-vs-short term-capital-gain-tax-rates.asp. Like ordinary income taxes, the tax you pay depends on your filing status, as well as your current marginal income tax bracket. The highest tax rate you'll pay is 20%. This is in comparison to a maximum rate of 37% when it comes to ordinary income taxes.

You can reduce your tax bill in several ways. This is

done by claiming deductions. Let's look at how this works.

Deductions

Deductions are exactly what their name suggests they are. They're items you can use to reduce your tax bill. There are two broad categories of deductions you can apply. The first is a standard deduction. Think of this as a discount that the government gives every taxpayer, free of charge. The standard deduction amount varies depending on your filing status. For 2020, here are the deduction amounts (Kagan, 2020):

- $12,200 for single taxpayers
- $12,200 for married taxpayers filing separately
- $18,350 for heads of households
- $24,400 for married taxpayers filing jointly
- $24,400 for qualifying widow(er)s

If you're single and are earning $80,000 per year, a $12,200 deduction in your taxes works out to a reduction of 15%, which is significant. Let's say you contribute the maximum amount of $19,000 into your 401(k) before taxes. This reduces your taxable income to (80,000-19,000) $61,000. Apply the standard deduction of $12,200 to this, and your taxable income is now (61,000-12,200) $48,800. Not bad at all! You'll be paying taxes on just a little more than half of your pre-tax income. Of course, you'll have to pay taxes on your 401(k) on withdrawal down the road, but you can grow that money for many years before paying taxes.

The standard deduction is chosen by most people when filing taxes because the other option, itemized deductions, doesn't always make sense. There are certain items that the IRS allows you to deduct from your income when filing taxes. The catch is that you can either itemize your deductions or claim the standard deduction. You can't claim both. For most people, their itemized deductions (of which you need to have records) don't add up to a greater amount than the standard deduction.

If you own property, this is unlikely to be the case. Here's why real estate is such a great investment. You can deduct practically everything that goes into maintaining your property, including your mortgage interest payment. Recall that you learned earlier that the monthly mortgage payment contains a principal portion and an interest portion. You can deduct that interest paid from your taxes. Therefore, your real expense is just the principal you pay your lender every month.

You can also deduct maintenance expenses, property taxes, mortgage insurance if you have any policies and other miscellaneous items. If you paid any local taxes (property taxes, for example), you could deduct these as well. There is a limit to the amount of local taxes you can deduct. You (or your accountant) will need to evaluate whether these individual deductions add up to a greater sum than the standard deduction. If it does, be prepared for the IRS to ask you for receipts and proof. This is why maintaining good records is essential—document everything.

Compared to real estate, stock market investments do not offer the potential for deductions. Dividends will be taxed as ordinary income. Capital gains will be treated accordingly, depending on how long you held onto the investment. Your broker will provide you with a Form 1099-DIV that will list how your dividends and capital gains should be treated. Your accountant will use this form to prepare your taxes.

Dividend taxation is complex, but I'm not diving into it for many reasons. For starters, it's irrelevant to you. You cannot control how your dividends will be treated. Secondly, your broker will identify how they ought to be treated on the 1099-DIV, so unless you have an academic interest in how they're treated, diving into dividend taxation makes no sense. If you are interested in understanding qualified versus non-qualified dividends, I suggest reading Investopedia or speaking to an accountant.

That's all there is to know about personal taxes. You contribute as much as you can pre-tax into your retirement accounts, claim either the standard deduction or an itemized list (with proof), and pay your taxes according to which ever tax bracket you land in.

BUSINESS TAXES

Business taxes are a bit more complex, but they can save you money. This is especially true if you have large business interests. Let's say you own more than ten properties and are collecting rent on them, or if you own an apartment block, it makes sense to own these investments through a company. The taxes you pay depends on your company's structure. Here are the three most common structures utilized by investors.

Limited Liability Company

The LLC is the most used business structure. The idea behind this corporate structure is that any liability claims that result from business malpractice are restricted to the assets that the business owns and don't extend to the owner's assets. Reads like a bunch of legalese, doesn't it? Well, here's an example to show you how it works. Let's say you own a restaurant, and some knucklehead decides to swallow a straw on purpose. They choke from it and almost die.

They sue you in court, claiming that you didn't warn them that swallowing the straw would be dangerous. The judge decides this is a reasonable argument and orders you to pay damages to the extent of $1 million for causing distress. Here's where the LLC protects you. If your business has assets worth $500,000, you don't need to pay them a dime more than this amount. If you don't have an LLC, the judge could order you to sell your assets, such as a rental property not connected to your restaurant or your investments in the stock market, to compensate the moron suing you.

I'm exaggerating the type of suit you could face in court. However, this sort of thing is extremely common in America and Canada. This is why every property you buy has homeowner's insurance. If someone trips on the sidewalk in front of your home and injures themselves, they might be able to sue you in court for damages. An LLC is a layer of protection and prevents people from targeting their assets. If you're rich enough, holding your prized assets in an offshore LLC can protect them from divorce settlements as well.

The great thing about an LLC is that its tax structure is simple. All income is treated as "passing through." In taxman-speak, this means the LLC itself doesn't earn anything. It simply receives all the money and passes them onto you. If you own an LLC, you'll need to file accounting statements with the IRS and then pay taxes on that income as a part of your income tax filing in April.

The downside of an LLC is that it makes business growth difficult. Let's say you own a restaurant through an LLC and decide that instead of paying yourself a salary, it would be better to reinvest those profits back into the business to earn more money down the road. With an LLC, you can't simply reinvest profits. You'll need to pay taxes on those profits and reinvest whatever is leftover. This makes business growth tough. This is why many business people prefer the corporation.

Corporations

Corporations are also referred to as C-Corps. They're treated as separate entities and aren't pass-through as LLCs are. They're living, breathing things, and need to be treated as such. You'll need to appoint a Board of Directors and elect officers. The board will need to meet at least once a year, and notes of that meeting need to be maintained. The corporation will file its taxes and profit and loss statements.

The IRS also stipulates that corporations need to pay taxes preemptively. This means that your accountant will need to project how much profit you can expect to earn and pay a certain amount of tax to the IRS every month. This amount paid is adjusted against your actual profit or loss at the end of the year, and the money is refunded, or you'll pay the balance. It takes a lot of time and effort to run a corporation.

The advantage is that since it's a separate entity, it can reinvest its profits as operating expenditures and not pay taxes on this. Your accountant, if they're honest, will warn you not to reinvest everything as operating expenses. Instead, they'll push you to classify the majority of expenses as capital expenditures or capex. Capex is the money you spend creating an asset for the business. Capex cannot be fully deducted; only a portion of it can be applied against income. The reality is that lines can blur between capex and operating expenses.

Let's say you invest in better chairs for your restaurants. Is this an operating or capital expense? Chairs can be considered inventory to deduct it from income like you would deduct the cost of buying food. However, chairs make your restaurant more attractive to customers and enhance your asset to be capex. Accountants need to make subjective judgments. To avoid getting into trouble, take the time to get to know the person's ethics, preparing your books. Stick to people who come recommended by others and have a stellar reputation.

You can pay yourself a salary every month from the company, whether it makes money or not. You don't want to pay yourself if the company isn't earning anything. This salary will be treated as ordinary income. The business will file its taxes, and you'll pay the amount due from its bank account.

S Corps

S corps are a combination of LLCs and C Corps. The problem with C Corps is that you'll pay taxes twice. The business pays taxes on its earnings, and you pay taxes on the salary you draw or dividends you pay yourself. The S Corp affords you the benefits of a corporation but has the pass-through nature of an LLC.

The money you pay yourself as salary (not dividends) can be deducted as business expenses, and you'll pay a reduced amount of taxes. Some clever people look at this as a license to deduct their entire profit as salary and find that the IRS comes down on them like a pack of hounds. S Corps are heavily scrutinized, and you need to make sure your accountant is a person of high ethics if you decide to go down this route. If any scandal ensues, you're the one who'll be in the spotlight, not them.

Using Legal Entities

The LLC is the most commonly used entity when it comes to athlete investments. They're easy to incorporate, and their taxes are simple. The key is to create a separate bank account for the LLC to separate your personal assets from your LLCs assets. You can invest in ventures using your LLCs money and will be protected from any liability claims. A good accountant will help you understand how you can protect yourself even more by managing your LLCs assets intelligently.

For example, you shouldn't place all your investment assets in an LLC. If you do get sued, you'll lose everything. It makes sense to set up different entities to hold different assets. Keep in mind that when it comes to real estate, banks do not prefer to lend to LLCs. They prefer lending to individuals. Most people apply for mortgages in their names and then transfer the property to their LLC. You'll need to take care of some legal formalities, so speak to your accountant about doing this.

If you've been following, your accountant is a crucial part of your tax and business picture. Ask for references and only choose those professionals who have a high reputation. If you're using a personal financial advisor, ask them for references. Ask your teammates or other people who own businesses for references to good accountants.

A common question is, should you consult an attorney or an accountant? When it comes to business matters, consulting an accountant makes more sense. This doesn't mean an attorney can't help you. Many athletes conduct their business through an attorney who manages all of their interests. Suppose you employ an attorney to handle the legalities of your businesses. In that case, you're outsourcing the choice of accountant and business ventures to them. If you can afford the services of one, it makes sense to do this. If you prefer a more hands-on approach, choosing to work directly with an accountant makes sense.

When it comes to tax affairs and company matters, the lines can blur between both professionals, so choosing either one makes sense. Just make sure they're highly reputable and have a high standard of ethics. Do not choose your close friends to represent you just because you know them well.

CHAPTER 7

LEGAL HELP, ATHLETE IMAGE ENTITIES, AND FINANCIAL ADVISORS

Laws are like cobwebs, which may catch small flies, but let wasps and hornets break through.

—JONATHAN SWIFT

AS AN ATHLETE, your image is your most treasured asset. In the past, bodies such as the NCAA used student-athlete images to earn billions of dollars. However, they treated the athletes themselves as indentured workers. This is changing, and it opens many athletes to the existence of athlete image entities. These entities are companies, much like the ones you learned about in the previous chapter, with the difference that their assets are intellectual, not physical.

Famous athletes utilize this arrangement all the time. Let's say Nike wishes to use LeBron James' image for their campaigns. They pay James' company a sponsorship fee and pay him royalties for the right to use his image. The company that holds the rights to license James' image is separate from the one that collects his sponsorship payments, to protect his assets from being exposed to a liability suit.

The way it works is that your image and everything connected to it, such as your social media accounts and any other intangible thing contributing to your image, is treated as intellectual property (IP). The IP is transferred to a firm. This might be hard to visualize, but it's all paperwork. You're the company owner, and the IP is just a bunch of paperwork that defines what the IP is.

Suppose anyone wants to use your image or its likeness, along with any signature phrases or anything else associated with you. In that case, they'll have to pay you license fees. This is why athletes are so conscious of their image in public. Famous athletes earn much money by licensing their images. If they speak out in public about controversial issues, they lose much money from the companies paying them licensing fees. Celebrities such as actors and reality TV stars use this tactic as well.

Often, phrases can be trademarked as well. This doesn't always work out since the trademarking language is tricky. A good example of this occurred in the previous decade when reality TV star Paris Hilton tried to trademark her signature phrase, "That's hot." A judge ruled that this amounted to trademarking the English language. However, her request was granted, and the use of this phrase in certain situations and on certain products such as clothing, electronic devices, and alcohol is trademarked (Protecting the Money Maker: 5 Celebrity Trademarks, 2020)

There have been athletes who have tried to generate additional cash through their name changing stuns. The former NFL wide receiver Chad Johnson changed his last name to "Ochocinco" and trademarked a logo around the name. Joel Embiid, the NBA player, trademarked items that refer to "The Process," Shaquille O'Neal has trademarked the phrase "Shaq Attack," Jeremy Lin "Linsanity," and so on. All of these trademarks are owned by image entities and constitute the IP that these companies own.

In the previous chapter, I addressed whether you need to approach a lawyer or an accountant to form companies. In the case of athlete image entities, a lawyer is the one you want to approach since trademarking and IP creation falls under the legal umbrella. It's helpful to set up an initial consultation with a reputed law firm to determine whether setting up such an entity makes sense for you.

LEGAL HELP

If your profile is big enough to warrant it, hiring a law firm to handle your affairs is a good move. How do you know if your profile is high enough? For starters, do you have local firms chasing you to sign sponsorships? If yes, then you have a high profile. Many people target athletes and their money. The minute your image is out in public, you need to start protecting yourself.

A law firm can provide you with a wide range of assistance. Let's look at some of the services these firms offer.

Real Estate Services

A critical part of your real estate investments are the leases you'll sign. The lease is a legal agreement that governs your relationship with your tenants. At some point, you're going to have to deal with a painful tenant who creates problems for you. You'll need to follow the procedures as laid out by the law and ensure you don't violate your tenant's rights in the process. Doing so could result in even more delays and a cash flow hole for you.

A good law firm will walk you through your lease's specifics and help you understand how you can structure it to protect yourself as an owner or as a tenant. Athletes need to lease temporary places all the time, thanks to spring training and offseason camps. Some of these leases can be tricky, so it's best to use expert help.

Financing and the mortgage application process are also tricky situations to navigate. You need expert legal help to find your way through it. It especially makes sense the first few times since you're unlikely to be familiar with how the process works.

Litigation

As an athlete with a profile, you are a target. People will sue you for stupid reasons to drag your name through the mud in the hopes that you'd rather settle than proceed to court and have embarrassing claims come to light. It isn't just issued that surrounds your playing career but other issues such as tenants suing you for weird reasons, financial advisors potentially entangling you in bad situations, and so on.

Having a good law firm by your side acts as an insurance policy. The people who serially sue famous people are aware of the law firms' reputations connected to their targets. Hire a strong law firm, and these freeloaders usually back away from you.

Corporate Services

Suppose you're going to be investing in and protecting your assets. In that case, you will need to form entities that do so effectively. Not only will you need to set up the right kinds of entities, but you'll also need to distribute your assets optimally between all of them. The services of a reputed law firm will help you figure out the maze of legalities you'll need to take care of.

You'll also need to handle legal matters related to the companies you set up, such as signing corporate charter papers and filing minutes of meetings. You can do all of this by yourself, but this will likely cut into your training time. It's best to outsource this to competent lawyers who can help you with everything.

Family Law

Athletes get divorced all the time, and other prickly family issues often arise when money enters the picture. Issues such as child custody, support, and divorce are sensitive issues. You don't want any of this spilling into the public eye, thereby damaging your image. A good law firm will help you navigate these muddy waters easily.

Taxes and Estate Planning

As I mentioned in an earlier chapter, you need to start planning for retirement during your playing days. You can't kick the can down the road and hope to pick the issue up later. A good lawyer will help you set up trusts, and other vehicles that can safeguard your wealth and will ensure your assets are disposed of in the manner you desire.

Take your time to hire a good lawyer. The right lawyer or law firm will be your greatest asset since they'll make several things simple for you. Once again, don't hire the person who's close to you just because of their proximity. Evaluate whether they're truly qualified to run your assets and advise you.

EVALUATING FINANCIAL ADVISORS

Professional athletes are often bombarded with recommendations for financial advisors. Using an advisor is a good move if your finances intimidate you or unsure how a particular investment opportunity works. It would help if you were wary of financial advisors. This isn't because they don't know what they're talking about or because they're incompetent.

They tend to lack personal experience with large sums of money and are not good business people. For example, a financial advisor would have never signed off on an investment such as LeBron James' Blaze Pizza investment. They would have instead recommended he place that money in bonds or stocks.

The issue isn't necessarily with the advisors themselves. There's also a problem in how society views their services. We expect them to know everything about money and expect them to evaluate every business opportunity with aplomb. If they truly had this ability, they'd be billionaires themselves and wouldn't be dispensing financial advice. The solution is to utilize its services effectively.

You can do this by asking them how an investment product works and telling them to explain its pros and cons in great detail. Do not be swayed by the way they look at risk. Every individual has their definition of risk, and their definition is not necessarily yours. The risk ladder that I presented previously in the chapter on investments, which went from real estate to the stock market to private businesses, is enough to help you determine how risky a business opportunity might be.

Once they've described the pros and cons to you, check whether you understand how the opportunity works. If you don't understand it, move on and wait for something else to come knocking. Remember that you won't miss out on huge opportunities if you forego a few. If you choose to stay away from opportunities you don't understand, you're not missing out on anything. Would you expect an engineer to perform the duties of a surgeon? Is the engineer preceding a golden opportunity if they elect not to perform surgery on someone? Of course not.

Here is an easy process that will help you figure out whether an advisor is worth your time.

Preliminary Work

Take some time to figure out your financial goals. It could be as simple as "I want a million dollars in the bank," or it could be more sophisticated as "I want to set up a trust fund for my kids and an annuity for my partner and I in 25 years." Write all of these down. Also, write down the things you understand about finance and investment and the things you don't.

Whether you know it or not, you have financial skills. Skills such as budgeting and getting rid of debt are all about habits. As long as you have the strength to follow the habits that will help you stay on track, they're easy to do. Investment skills require work. This is why I suggested a very simple investment template for you. Stay away from investing in individual companies because you need a host of other skills to do this successfully.

Lastly, examine your expectations. Markets don't always go up. It's easy to make money in rising markets. Markets that decline are what separate the wheat from the chaff. You cannot expect your investments to increase in value constantly. There will be times when you'll make a sound investment only to see your investment has declined in value. Remember that you aim to remain invested for more than 15 years at the very least. Fix these correct expectations in your head and drive the incorrect ones away. Check to see if you're trying to get rich(er) quick. Those schemes always lead to losses.

Questions to Ask an Advisor

The first question to ask is whether they get paid

commissions based on the products they recommend. Every advisor gets paid commissions for recommending certain mutual funds or investment products. Honest advisors let their clients know and discuss all the options on the table. Dishonest ones might not disclose commissions or might disclose it but not provide you with any other alternatives.

Ask them what their fee structure is and what your all-in costs are. Most advisors charge a percentage of the assets they manage. This is usually one percent. An important question to ask them is what kind of tax bill you will face by investing with them. Some advisors might trade over the short term frequently. While this will earn you a profit (or it might not), you'll pay far higher taxes. Stick to advisors who espouse a long term view of 15 years or more.

Check to see if they've hired a custodian for your money. A custodian is a brokerage firm that holds your funds in an account under your name. Some financial advisors act as their custodians and hold clients' money in their accounts. These kinds of advisors are almost always charlatans, so don't trust them. A financial advisor is not a hedge fund manager. They should not be holding your money for you.

Speaking of hedge fund managers, you need to recognize what realistic market returns are. Any business that returns 15% or more on the amount of money invested is exceptional. There are very few businesses in the world that will bring you this kind of return. If you invest in a restaurant franchise, you can expect around 7-10% as annual returns. I've already listed the average return you can expect with a stock market investment.

Real estate returns are very high, but this is because you'll be borrowing most of the money you need to buy a property. If you buy a property for cash, you can reasonably expect between 7-10% returns every year from the rental income. I'm detailing these numbers because you might have someone slide up to you and propose a venture that returns 20% per month. These are ridiculous numbers, and it's impossible to generate such returns. If these returns were true, Jeff Bezos is probably better off selling his Amazon shares and investing in this venture.

Ask your advisor what they think about certain businesses to get a feel for their risk tolerance. The objective isn't to see whether they give you a right or wrong answer. Instead, it's to see how conservative they are. This might sound odd, but you want to go with an advisor who is more conservative than you. This will prevent you from overextending yourself, and you'll always have a voice that counsels caution. This is very important when evaluating an investment since it can be easy to get caught up in your narrative and ignore counter-evidence.

If you are entrusting all of your money to the advisor, notice how they talk about generating investment returns. If they promise to double your money in a year or some such nonsense, run away from them. It doesn't matter if they've done this with someone else; you won't be missing out on anything by investing with such a person. If they promote some secret sauce or present themselves as being a genius, run away. Choose a person who is normal and is downright boring. This person will never leave you sleepless at night, worrying about the state of your money.

Ask them what their benchmarks are. A benchmark is a scale you can compare their performance to. Most advisors will choose the S&P 500. Underperformance in good years isn't always bad as long as they consistently outperform in bad years. Ask them for their track record and question them about it. Ask them which strategies they pursue, what asset allocation they followed, and why they underperformed. Remember, underperformance or losing money in a year or even two years isn't a bad thing. You want to see how honest they are about their mistakes and the lessons they've learned.

Trust your instincts and see whether you like them as a person. More often than not, this will alert you to situations that are too good to be true.

AFTERWORD

Despite what your advisors and those around you might say, always remember that it's your money. You're the one in charge, and you have the final say-so when it comes to making investment choices. You're also in full control of your budget and debt levels. Remember the lessons about creating an asset versus a liability and aim to create as many assets as possible. Minimize your liabilities and stay away from stupid decisions. This alone will ensure you'll take the right steps when it comes to your finances.

Throughout this book, my mission has been to empower you to make your own decisions. If you feel less than capable, seek help. I've given you helpful pointers on how you can evaluate the quality of such help as well. You don't necessarily need to hire a financial advisor to be successful with your investments. However, it would help if you made the right decisions. If you feel as if you can't do this, seek help. If you can, then view everything from the standpoint of risk.

Risk evaluation comes down to this: If the investment doesn't work out, how much of a hole will you be in? What is the likelihood of the investment not working out? For example, if a stock market index investment doesn't work out, you'll likely be in a big hole since you'll be investing much money into it. However, the likelihood of it not working out, in the long run, is slim. Hence, you can justify placing much money into it.

A private business has a higher chance of going belly up than the entire stock market. Therefore, invest a small amount of money into it and take more time understanding everything about it. Plan your taxes and other legalities well, and always remember to plan for your retirement, both of them. I wish you all the prosperity in the world.

WHAT'S NEXT?

Get excited for more books! Each day, I spend up to two or three hours planning, writing, and preparing my next few releases. In the meanwhile, I would love to hear your feedback about this book—I personally read every single review!

If you have three minutes to help me out, can you please post a short review on the platform from where you purchased this book. Thank you for your continued support.

Hadley Mannings

ALSO BY HADLEY MANNINGS

Athlete Habits

SOURCES AND BIBLIOGRAPHY

One of my goals for this book is for it to be as lean and as concise as possible. I would love to include my references and valuable resources, however, due to page limitations, I have uploaded this list online. For anyone wanting to access this list, please email:

hadleymannings@gmail.com

www.ingramcontent.com/pod-product-compliance
Lightning Source LLC
Chambersburg PA
CBHW021441080526
44588CB00009B/628